Prayers from Chautauqua

JOAN BROWN CAMPBELL

FOREWORD BY
SISTER JOAN D. CHITTISTER, OSB

The Pilgrim Press
Cleveland

DEDICATION This book is dedicated to the entire Chautauqua community,
both the religious and the not so religious. For fourteen
years I have been privileged to be your pastor. Those years
have been challenging, nurturing, satisfying, and richly
rewarding. I shall be forever grateful to those who count
Chautauqua as their spiritual home and those who have
given leadership throughout Chautauqua's 140 years.

SFI® Certified Sourcing
www.sfiprogram.org
SFI-00453

The Pilgrim Press, 700 Prospect Avenue, Cleveland, Ohio 44115
thepilgrimpress.com
© 2013 by Joan Brown Campbell

Scripture quotations, unless otherwise noted, are from the New Revised
Standard Version of the Bible, © 1989 by the Division of Christian Education
of the National Council of Churches of Christ in the United States of America,
and are used by permission. Changes have been made for inclusivity.

Hymn text (pages 6–8): "Stewards of Earth," text by Omer J. Westendorf
(1916–1997), copyright © 1984, World Library Publications, wlpmusic.com.
All rights reserved. Used by permission.

All rights reserved. Published 2013

Printed in the United States of America on acid-free paper

18   17   16   15   14   13   5   4   3   2

A catalogue record for this book is available from the Library of Congress

ISBN 978-0-8298-1985-4

contents

List of illustrations*

*All photographs were taken by Jeanne Wiebanga, MD, except that of Joan with Elian Gonzales and family, taken by Katie Campbell Morrison. Used by permission.

✳ foreword ✳

Prayer is a topographical map of the soul. The way a person prays signals the degree of breadth and maturity that underlies the spiritual life she or he brings to it. It's the prayers we say that expose to the world the mountains of life up which we've climbed, the gullies of growth through which we've walked on our way to wholeness. It is the inimitable sign of the values we bring to life and the people for whose cares we care.

To chart what a person prays for, then, is to follow the tracks of life that person has trod. "When I was a child," Paul reminds us in 1 Corinthians 13:11, "I thought as a child. . . ." Right: And I prayed as a child, too—short on depth of soul, long on longing for things.

But life has its way of growing us beyond the fancies of spiritual childhood to the gross realities of what it means to be a spiritual adult: To what it means to grapple with the darkness of depression, the challenges of disappointment, the awareness of injustice, the grip of pain, the fears of loss, the emptiness of death, the real beauty of life, the demands of its every stage and the spiritual message of its every season.

Indeed, it's the prayer tracks we've walked in from one stage of life to another that mark the growth phases, the concerns, the commitments, the struggles, and, finally, the sensitivities of soul that simply being alive has etched in us. In the end, it is the nature of our prayer life that is the one valid measure of our spiritual maturity.

A person's prayer is the measure of the heart of a person. We can hear in prayer where the human heart finds its heights and at what lows it has crossed its gorges only to rise to another level of life—wiser, clearer-eyed, more understanding, more caring, more abandoned to the ever loving will of God.

This book is living proof of all of that. It is a collection of prayers that mirror both the aspirations of a great national vision but also the commitment of that nation to be a genuine interfaith community—to be touched by one another's hopes and fears, by one another's needs and gifts, by one another's spiritual insights and moral perspectives. Most of all, these prayers lead a people of diverse traditions to become, at the same time, one spiritual community grounded in reverence and respect for the vision of the other in ways that deepen and grow our own.

Chautauqua Institution was founded in 1874 to make faith a living thing in a pluralistic society. And over the next century and more, true to itself and its vision of one America under God, Chautauqua developed beyond its own founding Protestant tradition to recognize, embrace, and learn from every faith while enabling every other faith to be true to itself.

Nothing is more reflective of that great vision than these prayers themselves.

All of these prayers were said in public worship at the Chautauqua Institution over a period of fourteen seasons, during years of great personal conversion as well as great national struggles to put down racism and sexism, religious separatism, and internecine political wars.

Joan Brown Campbell, director of the Department of Religion and chaplain of the Chautauqua Institution from 2000 to 2013, led the Sunday worship of this diverse community during this period. It is her prayers that shaped the heart of this many-faceted community. It is her pastoral presence that stamped the Institution as open to the entire human community, as citizens of the world, as truly Christian in every truly spiritual interpretation of the term.

Joan Brown Campbell, a woman born to be a pastor, has the kind of universal soul that broadens the spirit of those to whom she ministers. Literally thousands have had their hearts expanded, their souls deepened, their very outlook on life become softer and fuller because of her own. And it is her prayers that, like all of us, give her away.

In this book, the Reverend Joan prays for the kind of vision that always and in all circumstances takes in the others most unlike us, that saves the earth we overlook, that sees life as a seasonal process in which we grow from one age to another, always grappling with its lessons, forever resurrected by its unseen, unknown, and unexpected gifts.

She prayed people through their periods of personal loss, the Chautauqua community through its growth periods, and the nation through its struggles to be free and just, just and open, open and secure.

She demonstrated, as no manual of prayer possibly can, that prayer is not a device, it is a way of life, an attitude of mind, a development of the soul becoming ever more God-like, always more loving, forever more true to what it means to be a fully human human being.

"Prayer does not change God," the Danish philosopher Sören Kierkegaard wrote. "Prayer changes the one who prays." No work proves that insight better than this one.

These prayers come from the soul of one who has already been changed by them. They are an excursion through holiness, which, if prayed with care and consciousness, can only stretch our own souls to the limits of the presence of God within us.

May you find in them and make your own, the balm, the blessing, and the stark but softening reality of what it means to be a truly holy person.

Sister Joan D. Chittister, OSB

acknowledgments

No book is ever written without the help and encouragement of many who, all too often, go unnamed. Knowing that I cannot name all those who inspired this book of prayers, let me acknowledge those whose contributions were beyond any words I might offer.

The Chautauqua congregation that has inspired me over my fourteen years as pastor deserves a warm word of thanks.

Jared Jacobsen, gifted organist, choir director, and planner of worship was my companion in the planning and execution of the services of worship for the entirety of my tenure at Chautauqua.

Joyce Jacobson Brasted served as editor for this book. She patiently reviewed every prayer and is the one to be credited with a fine finished product. And, in her name, I thank her husband, Scott Brasted, and his gifted mother, Elaine Brasted, for their insistence on excellence.

Dr. Jeanne Wiebenga, medical doctor and gifted photographer, studied the prayers and helped give them inspiration through her beautiful photography. Her dedication to this book was unwavering.

Jane Louise Campbell, dedicated public servant, my oldest child and only daughter, dared to be honest with me, especially about which prayers to choose that would touch a diverse audience. Her hours of matching prayers and photographs are deeply appreciated.

Nancy Roberts and Maureen Rovegno gave me the time to write this book. Without complaint they carried more than their share of the daily work so that I might have time to write. I am grateful for their loyalty and emotional support.

Rabbi Samuel Stahl and his wife, Lynn, regularly attended the Chautauqua Christian services and inspired the interfaith character of many of the prayers.

Tom Becker, president of the Chautauqua Institution, offered encouragement from idea to finished product. I am grateful for his leadership and willingness to allow his staff to offer their gifts to a wider world.

Geof Follansbee, you offered friendship and encouragement, and I thank you.

Thank you all.

Note about the denominational books of prayer and worship: I am deeply indebted to those who, through the years, prepared the books for the Disciples of Christ, for the Episcopal Church, for the Presbyterian Church, for the World Council of Churches, and for the Jewish community, and especially to the United Church of Christ, whose eloquent Book of Worship inspired much of my writing. These became ecumenical resources for my prayers, and I am grateful!

introduction

THE ECUMENICAL CONGREGATION

When I arrived at Chautauqua in January of 2000, I soon realized that, although my title was director of the Department of Religion, I was, in reality, the pastor to a large and denominationally rich gathering of lifelong learners. Three thousand–plus people gather every Sunday, for ten weeks, to worship in the historic, outdoor Amphitheater. The congregation is diverse in every way. They are multidenominational and ecumenical in the most profound sense. The Chautauqua congregation is not dissimilar from congregational life throughout our country. The rich mix of denominational history and background invites an approach to worship that honors the richness of the gathered worshipers. Thus prayer became the hallmark of the ecumenical character of the Chautauqua congregation. So I offer these prayers to a wider audience in the spirit expressed by Sören Kierkegaard and quoted in Sister Joan Chittister's beautiful foreword, "Prayer does not change God; prayer changes the one who prays."

The prayers offered in this book address many of the burning issues of our time in history but they are deeper in content than that. They are prayers for the human condition common to all God's children the world around. The prayers draw on our shared ecumenical history as well as our deepening interfaith and international encounters. It is in our prayer life that we embrace the diversity and unity of all humankind. It is when we bow our heads and offer our hearts that we risk the surprises that await us when we open ourselves to God's will for our lives. I offer you a prayer, taken from the United Church of Christ Book of Worship, that inspired me and sets the tone for the prayers that follow.

Gracious God,
We confess what seems always with us:
Broken things within us that seem never to mend,
empty places within us that seem always to ache,
things like buds within us that seem never to flower.
O God of love and grace,
help us accept ourselves;
lead us to do those good and true things
that are not compromised by anything within us.
As much as can be,
mend us, fill us, make us bloom.
For all these things, we will give you the glory;
in spite of our tendency to pull apart,
in spite of our tenacity to our old ways,
our loving God continues to call us back together again.
Showing us the true nature of forgiveness,
God does not keep score of our wrongs or
    measure how far we have wandered.
God welcomes us.
We are forgiven people.

❋ I ❋

IN THE BEGINNING—CARE FOR CREATION

Dear Mother Earth,

I look outside my window at a beautiful, clear, and sunny day. Even though it is still winter, signs of spring are in the air. Once again, I realize that the miracle of the changing seasons is but one of your many gifts to us. Your care-filled concern for the well-being of all creation is eternally evident.

Mother dear, I write with heavy heart as I think of your children's limited appreciation for the life-sustaining gifts you have so generously provided us. You are the placenta that nourishes us. You cradle us without reservation and yet we take you for granted and fail to remember that you are the life force that sustains us.

With a profound sense of anguish, I realize how we have become separated from you and go our own way as though we alone matter. We walk the earth with a heavy step and believe that we are self-sufficient. I pray that this day may be a new day. As one of your children, I pray that this day may open many to a renewed awareness of the interconnection of all life.

We, your two-legged creatures, often claim a superiority that blinds us to our dependence on the interconnected web of water, land, plants, birds, and our four-legged companions. We are all one in our life's journey. The groaning of creation can be heard only if we are willing to listen to the world's people whose lives more directly depend on the daily gifts of sea and land for survival. Our possession-filled lives create a barrier to our understanding and appreciation of the source that sustains us.

So, dear Mother Earth, on behalf of the children you hold as precious, we confess our blindness to your pain and suffering as we carelessly use and abuse the treasures created for our well-being. May this be the beginning of a deepened relationship that is worthy of your life-giving love. Grace and peace.

✛

Creator God,
God of justice and grace and mercy:
 You have always called your people out of the darkness
 into marvelous light.
 You invite us to set aside a world of hurt and hopelessness
 and to join you as co-creator of a world of promise and possibility.
 You urge us to risk—even to fail—looking toward a future
 that is beyond our knowledge.
So with gratefulness and humility
 we pray for guidance as we risk setting forth our best
 and our boldest ideas.
 We do so in full recognition that your future will always be marked
 by a lavish love for the whole of creation for every child molded
 in your image.
All of nature sings your praises.
 With humility we pray for the insight, the imagination,
 and the courage to follow your way.
All who have walked the grounds of this place we lovingly call
 Chautauqua are touched
 by its beauty and almost all surprise themselves as they quietly,
 some with embarrassment, declare their experience spiritual.
We pray for a holy passion to claim minds and hearts as we move
 toward a future
 where success is measured by the finest in values.
 With gratitude we receive the many gifts that have been entrusted
 to our safe keeping.
Grant us courage for the living of these days.
Amen.

✠

Creator God,
>We stand in awe of the magnificence of all you have created,
>>all that ever has been, all that is, all that ever will be.
>We praise ourselves for our innovations, our inventions,
>and our discoveries.
>We look back over the years and are amazed at the world
>in which we live, work, dream, and dare.
>Rarely do we realize that all this is your created order.
>We are but those who discover what you already know.
>All you ask of us is that we tend what you have created
>>with justice and mercy,
>>tenderness and compassion.
>We live in a time when the whole world is in touch.
>We can communicate from outer space to the ocean depths.
>We can carry on conversations from teeming cities to remote villages.
>Are we in touch?
>Are we really allowing the lives of others to reach our hearts?
>Remind us that information sharing is not the same
>as the human embrace.
>Can we strike a cord within us that connects us to the needs of a world
>>where hunger persists and wars rage and women sit in the shadows?

God of all humanity, all creation, all that is yet to be discovered,
>we pray today for ourselves, we who are blessed
>with security and plenty.
>Stir in us a caring that is as global as our capacity to communicate.
>You have given us the insight and the imagination to connect
>to worlds unknown to us.
>We pray for the courage to explore our inner space,
>not just our outer space,
>>for the wisdom to use our new connectedness for justice and mercy,
>>for a tenderness to recognize in the miracle of technology the potential

For a world where we are truly in touch and live together
>as children of light and hope.

✢

Creator God, artist of the universe:
>You create for your children the beauty found in change;
>summer's rich green becomes fall's yellow, rose, orange,
>and gives way to winter's white.
>We so often think we want life to be still, to be as we always
>have known it,
>to hold on to what stirs memories in our soul.
>We also rejoice in our ever-changing environment.
>We are thrilled and inspired by the bounty of the fall harvest.

Help us, O God, not to fear change but to receive it as your gift.
>Open our hearts that we might allow nature to teach us that change
>offers new beauty,
>>renewed energy, and the possibility to see life with new eyes.

Holy God,
>We acknowledge our blindness, our failure to see the pain
>in the world around us.
>In the quiet of these moments, we pray, open our eyes
>to the needs of your children everywhere.
>Where there is hunger, teach us to give sustenance.
>Where there is disease, inspire us to share our healing gifts.
>Where there is bigotry and prejudice, confront us
>with our hardness of heart.
>Where there is war and cruelty, open the eyes of all humanity
>to the vision of peace.
>In these deeply divided times teach us how to love, how to listen,
>how to heal, how to embrace.

This is our prayer on this beautiful sunlit day.

Loving God, you come to us and urge us to lay our burdens down,
to bring them to your altar of grace.

Today as we begin our cosmic prayer let us kneel before one
who can hear the heart of each of us—no wish too small,
no concern too insignificant—no sadness too profound—
no fear too deep.

We pray for all who are ill—whose lives are compromised by pain—
whose futures are in your hands.

Bring strength to those who care for the ill and, if it be your will,
grant life to each and peace to all.

Creator God, we pray for all creatures who share this world with us.
You prepared for your people a world of beauty that nurtures
our bodies and fuels our spiritual beings.

You instilled in our souls a creative urge that has birthed poets,
painters, dancers,
artists, musicians, and writers, preachers, actors, and teachers.

The dance of the cosmos is our joy-filled response to all you have
given for our recreation.

We know not how to thank you other than to give our respect
to all creation.

(Sing "Stewards of Earth" to the tune of "Finlandia."):

All praise to you, O God of all creation:
you made the world, and it is yours alone.
The planet earth you spun in its location
amid the stars adorning heaven's dome.
We lease the earth but for a life's duration,
yet for this life it is our cherished home.[1]

Generous God,
From the very beginning we were dependent on your
expansive hospitality.

---

1. Hymn tune: Finlandia, Jean Sibelius, 1899, arranged for *The Hymnal*, 1933. Text: Omer Westendorf, "Stewards of Earth," 1984, ©1984 World Library Publications, wlpmusic.com. All rights reserved. Used by permission.

You gave us a garden to tend—life-giving land that brought forth
food for our development.
You offered an intricate weaving of fish and fowl and fruit.
You stirred our imaginations with birds to teach us to sing and
oceans whose crashing waves were the first symphony ever heard.
When we failed to care for these gifts, even with your
broken heart you saved us,
built an ark, and, two by two, gave the world a second chance.
We pray today for the good sense to love mother earth
as you have loved us.

> *With wondrous grace you clothed the earth in splendor;*
> *with teeming life you filled the sea and land.*
> *Instill in us a sense of awe and wonder*
> *when we behold the bounty of your hand.*
> *Then when we hear the voice or bird or thunder,*
> *we hear the voice our faith can understand.*[2]

God of grace and glory,
You breathed life into each of us and liberated us
to make our own decisions.
You trusted your creation to our free will.
We have not always used your gifts of life wisely nor shown
our love for the universe that
you in your wisdom envisioned.
Yet you love us and rejoice when scientists and explorers
expand our horizons,
reach for the stars, and visit the planets and bring back the message
that we are but a small blue dot
amidst a cosmos beyond our imagining.
You are amused at our arguments about creation and remind us
that all that is, has been, or ever will be,
you hold in your loving arms.
You are our God—we are your people.

---

2. Ibid.

We pray for the wisdom and the courage to share all we have been given with all of your glorious creation.

> *To tend the earth is our entrusted duty,*
> *for earth is ours to use and not abuse.*
> *O gracious God, true source of all resources,*
> *forgive our greed that wields destruction's sword.*
> *Then let us serve as wise and faithful stewards*
> *while earth gives glory to creation's Lord.*[3]

Then let us serve as wise and faithful stewards while earth gives glory to creation's God.

---

3. Ibid.

ODE TO SPRING

The sun glistens off the lake,
the flowers bloom, the colors invite the artist's brush,
the ancient trees miraculously give birth again.
Age-old branches sprout lovely leaves,
spring opens doors closed to winter's cold
and our spirits sing a hymn of grateful thanks.

✛

God of the ages, of worlds seen and unseen, Creator of all that is,
We give you thanks for the countless ways that you come to us
and delight us,
exhort us and inspire us, welcome us and urge us
to be neighbors to each other in this our global dwelling place.
We thank you for this time apart from our daily lives:
a time to learn, to listen, and to assimilate the new things
that you have held in store for us for just such a time as this.
When we look up at the night sky,
we think of all that lies beyond our understanding and experience,
the intricacies of the universe and the possibility of worlds
beyond our own.
For all we know, there may be, even today, creatures joining in
praises and hallelujahs to you in languages that we have never heard.
When we walk among people who are like us and yet unlike us,
we marvel at the variety of your creation,
we glory in the diversity of life,
and we wonder what lies within the hearts of those who surround us,
whose worlds of history and decades of individual living
we cannot know but in part.
We pray for the community of our families and friends with whom
we share a most intimate life.

Kyrie, eleison; Kyrie, eleison; Kyrie, eleison

We pray now for the community of those who surround us,
new neighbors of every faith and spirituality,
all moving toward you at your own bidding and at their own pace.
Help us to learn from them, to listen to them, and to share in their
own individual joys and gradual growth.

Kyrie, eleison; Kyrie, eleison; Kyrie, eleison

We pray for those communities from which we have come,
the cities and towns, the states and countries that have nurtured us
and have become the lenses through which we view the world.
Let those places become beacons of light and openness
for those who dwell within them.

Help us to participate in their life, to share in their progress,
and to shape their futures in ways that speak of justice and peace.

Kyrie, eleison; Kyrie, eleison; Kyrie, eleison

We pray for the community of people all over the world
who seek you in countless and mysterious ways,
who fervently desire to draw near to you,
who hope in your steadfast love and abounding mercy,
and who listen for your voice through rituals and symbols that we
do not know or understand,
but which are bright and beckoning lights to guide them on their way.

Kyrie, eleison; Kyrie, eleison; Kyrie, eleison

We pray, O God, for our global community, where there are
neighbors whose lights of hope grow dim in the torrential rains
and winds of war,
of hunger and suffering, and of turmoil and corruption.
Wash away the pain and the confusion with the healing waters
of compassion, mercy, and justice.
Show us how to truly be their neighbors,
and to allow them to become ours in ways that we cannot plan
but which you will show us as we make it our intention
today to bring humankind ever closer together
in your reconciling love.

Kyrie, eleison; Kyrie, eleison; Kyrie, eleison

✢

God of mystery and majesty,
> We kneel before you in awe confessing that too often
> we believe that we know what only you can know.
> You laid the foundation of the earth and
> the morning stars sang together and all the heavenly beings
> shouted for joy.
> Your greatness is beyond our comprehension
> yet we must confess that we sometimes (perhaps too often) believe
> that we know what only you can know.
> We confess that we make decisions based on our limited vision—
> and the world suffers.
> We are stunned at the intricacy and interdependence
> of your creation and
> confess our failure to care for every creature even as you cared for us.
> We come to know you, God, most clearly in the depth
> of our experience.
> We begin to understand that greatest of all, O God,
> is the mystery of your love.
> We kneel before you confessing that too often
> we are in awe of your creation and confess our failure to care
> for every creature, even as you have cared for us.

Greatest of all, O God, is the mystery of your love;
> you love us even when we do not love ourselves,
> you call us out of the darkness of our despair; you remind us
> that we are yours,
> created for hope and joy—wired for compassion and tenderness
> and peace.
> Forgive us for our failure to accept the mystery of love.

✢

Loving God,
Because the world is beautiful
and beauty is a tender thing
and we are stewards of creation,
we need you, God.
Forgive us our unwarranted self-sufficiency.

Kyrie, eleison

Because our knowledge seems endless
and we do not know what we do not know,
we need you, God.
Forgive us our dependence on facts,
our failure to search daily for truth.

Kyrie, eleison

Because we can live without you,
and are free to go against you
and could worship our wisdom alone,
we need you, God.
Forgive us our false gods,
our failure to seek first your kingdom.

Kyrie, eleison

✠

PRAYER OF THANKSGIVING

Creator God, ultimate planner,
    thank you for the beauty of Chautauqua.
    Thank you for the lavish gifts of sky and tree, the wonder of water,
    your intricate design that values bats and breathes life into babies.
Creator God,
    we, your co-creators, are humbled by your expectation
    that our hands can be trusted with the precious raw materials
    that await our human touch.
    With grateful thanks for all who have sculpted Chautauqua
    into a place of beauty,
    with deep appreciation for all artists
    who have imbued Chautauqua with soul and spirit,
    make us bold and brave as we dare to dream a future
    rooted in the past,
    molded from the clay of hope,
    brought alive by the courage and dedication of present-day pilgrims.
Creator God,
    we are your finest creation.
    Stand by us as we strive to live into your vision
    of a world where your people are in love with each other,
    a world marked by justice, not marred by violence.
    Mold Chautauqua into a place that teaches peace.
    Amen.

God of love and life
God of pardon
God of vision
Day after day, the world around, we pray your kingdom come
    your will be done on earth as it is in heaven.
You call us to live out your kingdom vision here where we live
    and love and work and worship.
Forgive us when we focus only on heaven and fail to work toward
    your kingdom here on earth.

Lord, have mercy.

God, you created all that is, all that will ever be, every tree,
    every animal, every plant, every child.
Your creation goes beyond our capacity to know and understand worlds
    beyond our world.
You have carefully created a world that requires interdependence.
Forgive us for our inability to see life whole, to live as a precious part
    of a magnificent and peaceable kingdom.
Forgive us our penchant for division.

Lord, have mercy.

Jesus, facing death on the cross, you prayed not for your own life
    but our unity.
You prayed that we might be *one* so that the world might believe
    your message.
You knew that our boundaries and walls would never be a witness
    to your love.
Forgive us the division between our churches, our nations, the races,
    young and old, women and men.

Lord, have mercy.

Loving God, you created us for community.
You filled our earth with all good things.
You created us with the capacity to share, to be open to all.
    You created a world without boundaries.
Forgive us for the barriers built by hands, ingenuity.

15

Remind us of our moments when walls came down and peace broke out.
Love us until your kingdom comes.

Lord, have mercy.

Lord God, your holy scriptures sing with your kingdom vision,
  where weak hands are strengthened, feeble knees made firm,
  fearful hearts made strong, eyes of the blind opened and ears
  of the deaf unstopped.
When we fail to reach for this vision for a better world
  for all your creation,
forgive us for breaking your heart.

Lord, have mercy.

Amen.

✠

CALL TO WORSHIP

In mystery and grandeur,
we see the face of God.
In earthiness and the ordinary,
we know the love of Christ.
In heights and depths
and life and death,
the spirit of God is moving among us.
Let us praise God.

✠

✻ 2 ✻

ALL GOD'S CHILDREN

The following prayer was offered the week that the Chautauqua Institution focused on Cuba and Cuban families. My richest encounter with Cuban family life was with the family of Elian Gonzales. I was deeply involved in the return of Elian to his Cuban family. They are a strong family and I believe to this day that Elian's life has been rich and full, nurtured by loving parents and grandparents. It seems abundantly clear to me that families raise children, governments do not. Elian is now nineteen years old and about to begin his advanced studies. I am certain he will make a contribution to his country and possibly to ours.

The picture on the following page includes Elian and me with his father, Juan Miguel, and Elian's grandmother.

———⋯———

God of grace and God of glory, on your people, pour your power;
    Today we pray especially for families.
    We pray for families where love is shared,
    where children are nourished and treasured,
    where all are allowed to be themselves,
    where affection is everywhere apparent,
    where transgressions are recognized,
    where forgiveness follows hurt and the old are embraced
    throughout their lives.
    May these families give thanks for the enormity of the gifts they
    give to one another
    and may they offer their well-loved lives
    in service to a hungry, hurting, and war-weary world.
We pray for families in crisis—for families where illness or tragedy
    or loss or bitterness or well-nursed hurts mark their lives.
    We pray for healing, for justice, and for peace.
We pray for families caught in the web of war and poverty,
    where death comes to the young,
    where danger constantly stalks their lives,
    where love may be the only food that sustains them.
    Open our eyes to their struggle
    that out of our blessing we might seek ways to minister to their need.
We pray today especially for families separated from one another—
    divided by a history not of their making.
    We pray for Cuban families whose ability to reach out to one
    another
    is clouded by past hurts and suspicions and artificial barriers.
    We pray for Elian Gonzales.
    We pray for the day when borders are opened and
    love can flow freely.
    We pray for families everywhere who yearn for one another—
    let it be so.

We give thanks for all those who have embraced one another—
    who have created family ties where none existed—
    for the homeless who care for one another in the shadows
    of our streets,
    for foster children who are given hope and hugs from parents
    who have the capacity to call all children their own—
    for all who choose to be family to one another.
    We learn from them how to choose and cherish one another.
Now in the quiet of this moment we thank you, God,
    for loving us enough to make of the whole world a family.
    So let us reach across all the barriers that would divide us;
    let us risk being us.
    Finally we are bold to pray for our own families
    and are reminded of that which is precious among and between us.
    We pray for those who have lost loved ones.
    So we give thanks for their lives and pray for solace
    for those who still sob in silent moments.

✠

We pray for the peace of the world:
> O God of healing and hope,
> today is a time of clash and conflict, arrogance and overreaching,

we face again our capacity to fracture the global family
and break your encompassing heart,
> heal, and claim us for the works of healing.

Bring us new hope born of reaching across to those we see as enemies,
> and thereby becoming warriors for peace.

We pray for the tranquility of our nation,
Almighty God, ruler of all the people of the earth, forgive, we pray,
our shortcomings as a nation;
> purify our hearts to see and love truth;
> give wisdom to our leaders and steadfastness to our people;
> and bring us at last to the fair city of peace,
> whose foundations are mercy, justice, and goodwill,
> and whose builder and maker you are;

and now, oh God, you who come to us in our deepest suffering
and in our moments of irreverent joy,
> we are made bold by your care for us to pray for those
> nearest and dearest to us.

We pray for young people whose lives are before them,
who dare to dream of a world of promise and peace.
> Be with them in their yet unwritten journey.

We pray today for those whose hearts are heavy with the loss
of their loved ones.
We name those who have died.
> In doing so they live in our memory:
> We pray for those whose names we do not call,
> those we carry deep in our hearts.
> You hear all our prayers.
> You minister to us in our silence and grief.

Healing God, we pray for all who are lost and lonely—
those who have given up on life.
> Renew their spirit.
> We pray as well for those whose lives are compromised
> by illness and for those who care for them.

We ask you, loving God, to guide us on life's journey. We, like the
Israelites of old, need you to guide us by day and by night. We give
thanks for the biblical record that reminds us that you do take notice
of us. And so we are made bold to pray today.

For all who are just beginning life's journey—we pray for babies
everywhere, emerging from safe wombs of security, entering an
uncertain world. We give thanks for Chautauqua's children, little
legs that are just learning to run, eyes bright with hope, hugs that
melt the most reserved. In our joy we do not forget to pray for those
children whose journeys from the moment of birth are clouded with
horrors too difficult to comprehend—poverty, bigotry, war.

Inspire us to be your agents of hope and promise that every child might
at least be fed and housed and clothed and loved.

We pray as well, O God, for young people everywhere, for those whose
journey into the world of education and work, marriage and family
building has just begun. Grant to the privileged a conscience that
stirs within them and grants them the sight to behold your vision of
justice and peace. For those who face a world of poverty and despair,
watch over them, O God.

Life's journey takes us from birth to youth to our years of responsibility.
For all those of us in those middle years, where we learn life's
toughest lessons, where we wrestle with becoming who God
intended us to be, we are most in need of the pillar of fire by night
and the cloud by day that you, O God, set before us to assure that
we are not alone. We pray for parents, teachers, businesspersons,
dentists, doctors, carpenters, artists, single people, married people,
gay people, soldiers, and pacifists. Help us rejoice in our choices and
grant us the courage to change our ways if we have brought pain to
any, including ourselves. We pray now for us here in this place.

Finally, O God, we pray for those who come to the end of the journey,
the final road. Light the pathway to heaven and home. For your
constant gift of presence, for noticing us in our need, we are ever
your grateful people.

And now we pray the prayer that many of us learned in the
beginning of our journey:

(Say the Lord's Prayer in unison.)

God of Grace and Glory,

We come before you this day thankful for gifts that we took for granted. Electricity that pulses through the veins of our cities and lightens the evening sky and powers life-giving machines in our hospitals, water that so easily drains from our ever-plentiful faucets. We pray for those who have borne the burden of keeping us safe; for our mayors we ask rest for their weary bodies. We come mindful that for us to be without is rare and a newsworthy occurrence, but for many in this world—especially we think of those in Iraq and other war-torn places—the days are sweltering and nights too often dark. God, make us more fully mindful of one another's needs.

Creator God,

We come before you this day mindful of the great gift you have given to us, companions who walk this rocky road of life with us. Today we pray especially for families, for sisters, brothers, cousins, parents, grandparents, great grandparents, friends, partners, husbands, wives. We pray for ourselves today. We pray for intimacy in relationships, an intimacy that can only be when fear is swallowed up in love and passion is a risk we joyfully, playfully embrace.

Holy God, you have commanded and equipped us to love one another. Let it be so.

✛

Everlasting God,

We come before you once again to pray for all who are ill. We light a candle for their recovery. We pray for all who grieve. We light a candle for all who live in poverty, all who are homeless and loveless as refugees. We light a candle for all who wander and wonder what the future holds. And finally we light a candle for all who live in fear, for all who are burdened with anxiety, for all who have to be satisfied with who they are, what they have, and what they can accomplish. Grant them peace and the joy that comes from faith in a faithful God. Amen.

Great and Gracious God,

We come before you with humility as we acknowledge your limitless love, a love too deep for us to fathom, too wide for our reach, more inclusive than even our boldest imaginations can envision. We bow before you and pray to be a people ready to receive your love for us, ready to open our hearts to the world you created, willing to come to the table you have set, to sit with your guests as our sisters and brothers.

Kyrie, Kyrie, eleison

O God we live in a world often strange and difficult for those who believe. Our time, perhaps like all times, is unsettled and often called uncertain. And so, we are tempted to ask of you exaggerated things: interventions on our behalf even when they contradict who you are, O God, petitions aimed at making things right according to the way we measure. We ask you to stop quarrels and conflicts as if they were not our business, to deliver us from our overly stressful and often self-indulgent aspirations, to keep us safe no matter what we choose to do, and finally to use your mystic powers to make life good. How immature our believing can sometimes be! Lead us, O God, to pursue our faithfulness wisely, with well-schooled realism and with an openness to your spirit to guide us into what is true.

Kyrie, Kyrie, eleison

Help us to remember that you love all people with your great love, that all religion is an attempt to respond to you, that the yearnings of other hearts are much like our own and are known to you. Stir in church leaders and lay people alike a passion for unity. Remind us that you prayed your vision that we might be the one people we were created to be. Help us to recognize you in unlikely places and faces, in acts of loving-kindness. In words of truth, in the beauty that surrounds us.

Make us newly aware that love is the greatest force the world has ever known. Hatred has had its way with us too long.

Teach us the way of justice. Show us the path of peace.

Kyrie, Kyrie, eleison

And now, O God,

    We are bold to offer prayers for ourselves. For all who are ill, for those who grieve, for those whose families are torn apart, may their sleepless nights end and their lives be blessed with peace. For the searching, O God, we cease our talking and in the silence we await your presence in our lives.

    Our hearts have spoken, shed tears,

    revealed our sadness, our sorrow,

    yet in the midst of it all, somewhere,

    perhaps in a favella, maybe in an African village,

    possibly in a castle, surely in Chautauqua,

    a child's tiny finger reaches out and touch us,

    and hope springs forth,

    and our determination to create a peaceful world is renewed.

The spirit moves among us, and we are made whole again.

God of grace, love, and compassion,
>We confess that we have failed to love you
>with our whole heart and soul and mind.
>We ask ourselves, "How could that be, where did we lose our way?"
>>And so we pray:
>God, you whose love through humble service bore the weight
>of human needs,
>forgive us our foolish ways.

God of creation, you formed us in your image,
>humbly we confess that all too often we recreate you in our image.
>We confess that we limit our love and reach out only to those
>who look like us.
>As we worship grant us vision that we might see and embrace the needs
>and burdens your compassion bids us bear.

God of this world and worlds yet unknown,
>we confess that we name as neighbor
>only those whose world we know and understand.
>Forgive us our failure to name each of your creatures "neighbor,"
>rare treasure to be loved and protected.

Gracious God, you alone can probe the depths of the human heart,
>hear the prayer of the humble,
>and justify the repentant sinner.
>Grant us the gift of a compassionate heart
>that beats beyond boundaries
>and loves without limits.

✠

Holy God, we come before you humbly confessing our inability
to grasp your care for us.
    We awaken—only rarely—to the reality that you reside in our
    minds when you desire to occupy our hearts.
    We keep you at arms length.
    We write theological treatises about your being.
    We argue about your very existence.
    We struggle to understand the enormity of your being.
    We say familiar words disconnected from our deepest feelings.
    We confess that in all our thinking we miss your greatest gift—
    a boundless affection that can only be felt in our hearts.

Santo, santo, santo

God of extravagant hospitality,
    You created us for love, yet we tremble when love takes hold of us.
    We fear we have lost control of our carefully measured generosity.
    But you will not let us go—
    you surprise us with the wet kiss and the extravagant hug
    of a small child.
    Beyond all reason we are amazed at our out-of-control response.
    We love beyond all imagination.
You teach us to live in ways that challenge caution and
    we dare to explore the reality that love is unlimited
    and is meant to be shared.
    We confess we fear loves' power.
    So very carefully we open our hearts to your gift of love.

Santo, santo, santo

God of Hope and Promise,
    You hold the whole word in your embrace.
    Your reach touches every heart.
    Your language is understood by all people.
    Barriers and boundaries are not of your making.
    Even as we pray for peace we fail to trust in your promise
    that all can be made new.
    We confess that we are fearful of too much hope.

We do not wish to be seen as naïve in a troubled world.
Yet despite our hesitation you stir our hearts
and once again they beat with passion and we are grateful.

Santo, santo, santo

✟

Living Loving God,

We bow our heads and open our hearts to you as we confess aloud what you already know. We promise regularly that we will walk in the way you have set before us. We will love our neighbor. We will love ourselves just as we are not as we wish we were. We confess that we fall short of the promise we have made to you and to ourselves. So we pray (sing to the tune of Angel's Story):

O Jesus, I have promised to serve you to the end;
O give me grace to follow, my Savior and my Friend!

Compassionate God, Merciful One,

You have set before us in words of unmistakable clarity the marks of the Christian life. To preach good news to the poor, release to the captive, sight to the blind, food for the hungry. We cannot claim that the words are too complicated, that we do not understand their meaning. We know that these are the promises we must fulfill and yet we confess that our own agenda often takes all our lives and energy. Too often we promise ourselves we'll get to your way, but not yet. We know that your way is the way of peace, the way of justice, and so we pray and ask for yet another chance to keep our promise to you (sing to the tune of "Angel's Story):

O Jesus, I have promised to serve you to the end;
O give me grace to follow, my Savior and my Friend!

Eternal God, Immortal One

We acknowledge that you and you alone can see the future, that you and you alone hold the whole world in your hand. We confess that we are anxious about the future for those nearest and dearest to us and that we fail to see that our future is inexorably linked to the future of all humankind. We confess that in our busyness we fail to take time to see a future different than the one we ourselves can create. We fail to grasp the hope in your eternal presence, the hope inherent in placing ourselves as servants of your vision. So we pray:

O Jesus, I have promised to serve you to the end;
O give me grace to follow, my Savior and my Friend![4]

God of Wisdom and Truth,

Give us the courage to put our trust in your guiding power. Raise us out of the paralysis of guilt into the freedom and energy of forgiven people and for those who through long habit find forgiveness hard to accept, we ask you to break our bondage, set us free, mold us as keepers of your promises, O Jesus.

Sing the entire hymn "O Jesus, I Have Promised."

---

4. "O Jesus, I Have Promised," words by John E, Bode, ca. 1866; tune: Angel's Story, A. H. Mann, 1883.

Merciful God,
> You created us for love.
> We give thanks this day:
> For quiet acts of splendid courage,
> for mother and father, sister and brother,
> husbands, wives, partners, neighbors, friends
> who have through acts of heroic loving
> saved lives, quieted pain, provided healing laughter.
> Their compassion breeds hope in a world grown too easily cynical.

> > *O God, hear us, hear our prayer.*

Today we remember all those whom the world
> has crowned heroes and heroines.
They bear the burden of huge expectation,
> yet they wrestle with the knowledge of their own imperfection.
Help them not to take their press too seriously,
> and grant them the capacity to laugh.
Give them the gift of love from those who truly know them,
> that we are flawed, yet capable of glory.

> > *O God, hear us, hear our prayer.*

Eternal and Almighty God, Creator of ordinary people
equipped for extraordinary tasks,
> we give thanks for all your faithful people
> who have followed your will in a grand procession of praise
> throughout the world and down throughout the centuries,
> into our own time and place.
We hear their stories in the pages of scripture,
> in the records of history, in the recollections of our families,
> and in our own childhood memories.
As we remember these people, inspire us to rise to their ranks,
> to be bold as they were, and brave as well.

> > *O God, hear us, hear our prayer.*

Holy God,
> Whose ways are not our ways and whose thoughts
> are not our thoughts,

grant that your Holy Spirit may intercede for us
with sighs too deep for words.
We pray for all those whose loss of loved ones
still brings tears to the eyes
and renders the night hours lonely.

O God, hear us, hear our prayer.

✛

Baptismal Prayer

O God, we come before you in gratitude for this new life,
  embraced in the arms of her father.
This little child, so dear and precious, is the object of her parents' love.
She is the hope of the dreams of her grandparents and the
  guarantee of their immortality.
She is their promise of tomorrow.
We pray that this little girl may grow to be a woman,
blessed with good health of body and of mind.
May her parents, Jon and Peta, raise her, secure in their own love,
mindful of their own values, proud of their own place in the world.
They have declared this child's name to be Ava Davis Verhaege.
May Ava's name be honored in our community.
May Ava's body increase in strength.
May her mind expand with curiosity and wonder.
May her heart be filled with love.
As she now cries out for food and comfort,
may she, some day, cry out against the injustices of our world.
May every day of Ava's life, O God, be filled with love and compassion.
And may the blessing we offer her today remain throughout a long,
  healthy and worthy life.

*Note: This was a prayer for the granddaughter of Ann Noble, Joan's
longtime friend.*

 **3**

LIBERTY AND JUSTICE FOR ALL

God of yesterday, today, and tomorrow,
    Even in the darkest of moments, when life is fleeting,
        you bear us up on eagle's wings and hold us
            in the palm of your hand.
    You know our deepest sorrows, our secret sadness,
        our impossible dreams.
    We are your children, and you are our God.
    We come to you as your faithful people,
        people seeking peace,
            people seeking wisdom.

Oh God, hear us, hear our prayer.

God of every nation and all people,
> Every language is known to you,
>> every land was created by you,
>> every baby born is your child,
>> every death is your sorrow.
> You created us for love,
>> and you weep when hatred and terror,
>> recrimination and retaliation
>> take root in our souls.
> Oh God, stir in us a passion for peace.

Oh God, hear us, hear our prayer.

God of surprises and possibilities,
> you know us better than we know ourselves.
>> You know our capacity for love and compassion,
>> even when we do not recognize or respect it in ourselves.
>> You know our power and our might.
>> You know our temptation to misuse it.
>> Instill in leaders and learners alike a passion
>>> for mercy and justice.
>> Equip us for love.
>> Surprise us, oh God, with a yearning for peace.

Oh God, hear us, hear our prayer.

God of transformation,
> Take our sadness and our sorrow, our memories,
> our tears, our anger, our fears,
> mold them into a thing of beauty.
> Mark September 11 in the eternal calendar:
> A day when courage and love defended against evil.
> Let us remember it as the day when courage was born.
> Mold it into a thing of beauty.
> Send us forth a transformed people.
> Redeem our suffering and our darkness.
> Turn us toward the light of love.
> Teach us all the way of peace.

Infuse us with the power of forgiveness.
Hold before us the vision of a reconciled world.
Send us forth a courageous people, willing to risk it all
    for a world where peace is possible.

Oh God, hear us, hear our prayer.[5]

✛

---

5. Prayer for the Interfaith Service of Remembrance, Washington National Cathedral, September 11, 2002.

9-11-2006 PRAYER

Five years of remembering:

Death	Danger	Destruction
War	Enemies	Terror
Fear	Battles	Victories

Stir our memories, O God, that our remembrance might be our teacher.
  Life lessons will illumine our souls;
  emotions hatched out of bigotry and jealousy and war
  will give way to peace.
  The only victories that have eternal memory
  are victories that guarantee a future to our children.
    Life over death,
    love over hatred,
    peace over war,
    courage over fears,
    justice over bigotry,
    forgiveness over vengeance,
  embrace each other in love and peace.
  Our only security is in our surrender to your will and your way.
  Our hope is rooted in a passionate search for a peaceful tomorrow.
So, God of the ages,
  whose wisdom is beyond our imagining
  open us this day to remembrance of your love for all your children.
Amen.

✠

Prelude to the prayer: Week after week, I, along with Jared Jacobsen, organist and coordinator of Worship and Sacred Music at Chautauqua, meet to prepare for you—who bless us with your presence—a service that will touch your hearts, feed your souls, expand your minds, and foster courage and compassion. It seemed appropriate that as we focus on the presidency, we should pray for those whose decisions affect the whole world. A portion of the prayers of the people is taken from a prayer written in 1910 by the Rev. Dr. Walter Rauschenbusch, professor of Social Ethics at Colgate Rochester Seminary. The echoes from the past are incredibly relevant today.

Let us pray:
God, you who come to us in our great joys,
our crushing sorrows and in our lives day to day;
be with us now—as we open our hearts to you in prayer.
We pray today for all whose decisions affect the lives of many.
We pray especially for those who seek to give leadership
in service to the people of this great country.
We approach the time when we the people must discern the qualities
that might commend public officials to receive our support.
We come to a time when our decisions, not just those of our leaders, will
matter to the whole world that you, loving God, hold in your hand.
So we join those who went before us and shared their wisdom
and worry with us.

God, great governor of all the world, we pray for all who hold or seek public office and power; the lives, the welfare and the well-being of the people are in their hands to make or to mar. . . . Strengthen the sense of duty in our political life. Grant that the servants of the state may feel ever more deeply that any diversion of their public powers for private ends is a betrayal of their country. Purge our cities and states and nation of the deep causes of corruption which have so often made sin profitable and uprightness hard. Bring to an end the stale days of party cunning. Breathe a new spirit into all our nation. Lift us from the dust and mire of the past that we may gird ourselves for a new day's work. Give our leaders a new vision of the possible future of our country and set their hearts on fire with large resolves. Raise up a new generation of public men (and women), who will have the faith and daring of the Dominion of God in their hearts, and who will enlist for life in a holy warfare for the freedom and rights of the people.[6]

Great God of the ages,
　　Open us to the wisdom of those who have gone before
　　And stir our hearts to strive always for a world
　　Where all your children are fed and clothed
　　And housed and freed. Amen.

✠

---

6. Rev. Dr. Walter Rauschenbusch, professor of Social Ethics, Colgate Rochester Seminary, published in *The American Magazine* vol. 69/3 (January 1910), 434.

An Inaugural Benediction

As the nation prepared for the inauguration of President Barack Obama, Paul Raushenbush from *The Huffington Post* sent out a call that went like this: "If you were asked to give the closing benediction, what would you offer as a gift to President Obama?" The challenge was too great to pass up. Here is my prayer offering to our forty-fourth President. Thank you, Paul, for this challenge.

Eternal God,
    We come before you humbled by the gifts we have been given,
    painfully aware of the challenges facing our nation.
    On this inauguration day, bless your servant, Barack,
    with the wisdom and courage
    to face the future that demands no less from him than his finest hour,
    day by day.
    As people of many faiths, we acknowledge the burden
    of destructive divisions.
    So, we pray, open our hearts and minds
    to the unity of all humankind.
Holy, Immortal God,
    Be to President and people alike a beacon of light and love.
    Bless this nation with the unity that is your gift and your challenge.
    Amen.

✠

PRAYER FOR OUR NATION'S BIRTHDAY

Today as we celebrate the nation's birthday we remember all who are touched by this country's power, by our vision, and by our decisions. We pray for these United States on this week of our nation's birthday. We are a nation blest with waves of grain, majestic mountains, and fruited plains. We give thanks for your great gifts and pray for generous hearts that we might respond with compassion to a hungry, hurting, war weary world:

> *America! America! God shed his grace on thee,*
> *And crown thy good with brotherhood from sea to shining sea.*

Holy God: You created us for freedom. You called us out of slavery, out of darkness into your miraculous light. You sent among us pilgrims, prophets, peacemakers, who dared to dream of an America that would be to the world sign and symbol of life, liberty, and justice for all. We yearn for that America. Walk beside us, whisper that vision of hope in our ear again and again until America's flaws are perfected and liberty is laced with love and we claim the whole world as our neighbor.

> *America! America! God mend thine every flaw,*
> *Confirm thy soul in self-control, thy liberty in law.*

Merciful God: We give thanks for all who have gone before us, for all who have and continue to protect our freedom serving this great nation. For all who gave their full measure of devotion—presidents, poets, teachers, preachers, soldiers, pacifists, reformers, and conscientious objectors, and, on this our national holiday, we pray for strength in our quest for peace. Remind us that the heart for peace stirs in every nation and in all people everywhere. Freedom is your gift to all your children. It is a gift in which we rejoice. May we tend it tenderly (It is ours to share, not ours to impose on others).

> *America! America! May God thy gold refine,*
> *Til all success be nobleness and every gain divine.*

God of vision, who walks with us into the future, we pray for our alabaster cities stained with human tears. We pray for the day when misery will know relief, when war and bigotry are no more and mercy will mark all our dealings with one another. We pray today for the world's cities, their people and their leaders.

God of the ages, mold us as a loving people, people who live with extravagant love. Mold us into a healing nation inspired by the outreached hand of Lady Liberty, whose tear-stained face still dares to dream of America, where peace is possible, freedom is shared, and extravagant love will be the last word.

> *O beautiful for patriot dream that sees, beyond the years,*
> *thine alabaster cities gleam, undimmed by human tears!*
> *America! America! God shed his grace on thee,*
> *and crown thy good with brotherhood from sea to shining sea.*[7]

✛

---

7. "America the Beautiful," words by Katherine Lee Bates, 1893; tune, Materna, Samuel A. Ward, 1893. Prayer originally printed in Joan Brown Campbell, *Living into Hope* (Woodstock, VT: SkyLight Paths Publishing, 2010), 115–17.

How great is your love, Lord God, how wide is your mercy!
    Never let us board up the wide gate that leads to life with
    narrow rules or doctrines that you dismiss;
    but give us a Spirit to welcome all people with affection,
    so that your church may never exclude secret friends of yours,
    who are included in your all-embracing love.
God, good beyond all that is fair, in you is calmness, peace, and concord.
    Heal the dissensions that divide us from one another and
    bring us back to a unity of love bearing some likeness
    to your divine nature.
    Through the embrace of love and the bonds of godly affection,
    make us one in the Spirit.
    Give us the courage to engage, where the crying is too constant,
    where the good things of life are not shared.
We pray especially today for cities,
    for all who live and love and face life's burdens and blessings
    amongst the throngs who call the city home.
    We pray for cities around the world where life is lived lavishly by a few
    and whose struggle and sadness and disappointments
    mark the lives of too many.
We pray for Detroit and all the "Detroits" of this country,
    where yesterday's success is but a memory and
    the promises of tomorrow are just a vision.
    We pray for renewal for this and every city that seeks new dreams
    and new possibilities.
We pray for faithful people in all the cities
    that they might be symbols of light and love,
    wherever there is darkness and despair.
O God of healing and hope,
    Today is a time of clash and conflict, arrogance and overreaching.
    We face again our capacity to fracture the global family
    and break your encompassing heart.
    Heal,
    and claim us for the works of healing.
Almighty God, ruler of all the people of the earth, forgive,
    we pray, our shortcomings;

purify our hearts to see and love truth;
give wisdom to our leaders and steadfastness to our people;
and bring us at last to the fair city of peace,
whose foundations are mercy, justice, and goodwill, and
whose builder and maker you are.
For all your children the world around,
we pray that their lives might be marked by joy.
For all of us who are blessed with warmth and security,
may our hearts be opened as life is shared and hope is born.

✠

Gracious God,

You come to us in our great joys, in our crushing sorrows, and in our life day to day. We sense your presence in our midst, and in the loneliness of the darkest nights, your Spirit hovers and bids us come. We say, "Yes, Lord"; we pray, open our hearts to hope and take of our weakness and make us strong:

> *Love so amazing, so divine*
> *demands my life, my soul, my all!*

We come today grateful for the security that is ours in this place. We walk the streets, bask in the sunlight, cool ourselves in the shade of age-old trees, and dream beside the quiet of the lake and smile as children play with abandon.

We do not take this gift lightly but receive it as both blessing and challenge. Almighty God, we pray that the gifts of serenity and beauty that surround us will stir our hearts to reach with vigor and compassion to those for whom security is an unfamiliar experience, a seldom reality. Your love for all your children calls us to reach deep into our souls and find new energy for loving, forgiving, caring.

Help us to live as your people, to claim a history that rejects the seeds of war and famine, of greed and bigotry. Help us to live in the light of your love.

> *Love so amazing, so divine*
> *demands my life, my soul, my all!*

God of all nations, all people, we give thanks for the moments of peace in a century marked by violence. We give thanks for leaders who gave their lives to end oppression, for saints who dare to live nonviolently in a world where power too often rules by the sword. May these teachers and saints instill in us life lessons that move us to follow their way. And for the peacemakers in these days, strengthen their resolve. For leaders everywhere in all nations, and in all walks of life, grant them a vision of a world where love has the last word.

We give thanks for those events where good prevailed and courage was claimed and determined souls grew in damaged soil. Help us to learn from their tenacity, their determination, to make of the desert a garden of grace and mercy.

From these signs that your will and your ways have the last word we draw hope. Instill in us the vision to be agents of your agenda in our time and place. Help us to write a history of justice and mercy.

Now in the stillness of this moment, we implore you to disrupt our predictable lives and instill in us a yearning for the beauty of a world where the security of all is our hearts desire.

> *Love so amazing, so divine*
> *demands my life, my soul, my all!*

Great God, whose arms can hold both the whole world and each of us in your heart, we give thanks that those who have died are at peace in your eternal embrace. For those who grieve, may their tears meld with the joy of their memories.

Now for those among us whose bodies wait for healing, we pray for recovery, and if that is not to be, we pray for the peace that endures.

Gracious God, for hearing us, for knowing us and loving us always, we give thanks and join in the prayers for all your children.

Note: Sing the complete hymn "When I Survey the Wondrous Cross."[8]

✠

---

8. "When I Survey the Wondrous Cross," words by Isaac Watts, 1707; tune, anon.

Merciful God,

> We strike a match and our candle sparkles with light. We are
> reminded of our great promise—how every day the darkness is
> always dispelled, light always overcomes, and a new day dawns.
> It is in gratefulness for this hope that we kneel before you.

Merciful God,

> You come to us in our great joys, in our crushing sorrow,
> and in our life day to day. Be with us now as we pray for the
> blessing of your healing powers.

Loving God,

> Your healing powers walked the earth in the person of Jesus
> and your people were touched in miraculous ways.

> Through the ages the rough places have been made smooth
> and the broken hearts mended. We give thanks.

> So we are made bold this day to pray for our alabaster cities
> dimmed by human tears. Restore our cities that they might become
> for their people places of healing and mercy and justice. Strengthen
> those who lead our cities that they might find in your love, O God,
> the courage and compassion to transform our cities into places
> of learning and light.

> Open all our hearts, O God, that we might be freed of all fear
> and released as your people readied for service and sacrifice.

> We pray not only for our own cities but for the cities of the world.
> Your people live everywhere, and we are called to be neighbors to
> one another.

Holy God,

> Take hold of us, heal our fearful souls that we, your people the
> world around, might risk the way of peace. Remind us again and
> again that we are all your children and that unity is your gift and
> our challenge.

> Finally, knowing we are loved, each of us as though there were
> just one of us, we pray for those closest to us, for those we love
> and cherish.

We give thanks, eternal God, for those who have run the race of faith before us and now surround us like a cloud of witness.

We pray for all who suffer, for those whose prospects for recovery are dim, for those recovering from illness, and those who care for them. For all of these we pray, O God, for your healing mercies. We pray also for lives well lived.

We rest our weary souls in the assurance that there us a balm in Gilead:

> *There is a balm in Gilead to make the hurting whole;*
> *there is a balm in Gilead to heal the wounded soul.*
> *Sometimes I feel discouraged, and think my work's in vain,*
> *but then the Holy Spirit revives my soul again.*
> *There is a balm in Gilead to heal the wounded soul.*[9]

✛

---

9. "There Is a Balm in Gilead," African American spiritual based on Jeremiah 8:22.

Almighty God,
>Giver of all good things,
>we are bold today to pray for our nation.
>We thank you for the natural majesty and beauty of this land.
>They restore us, though we often destroy them.

Heal us.
>We thank you for the great resources of this nation.
>They make us rich, though we often exploit them.

Forgive us.
>We thank you for the men and women who have made this country strong.
>They are models for us, though we often fall short of them.

Inspire us.
>We thank you for the torch of liberty that has been lit in this land.
>It has drawn people from every nation,
>though we have often hidden from its light.

Enlighten us.
>We thank you for the faith we have inherited in all its rich variety.
>It sustains our life, though we have been faithless again and again.

Renew us.
>Help us, O Lord, to finish the good work here begun.
>Strengthen our efforts to blot out ignorance and prejudice,
>and to abolish poverty and crime.
>And hasten the day when all our people,
>with many voices in one united chorus,
>will glorify your holy name.

✛

God of all nations,
God of our nation,
    We come before you as your grateful people.
    For over two hundred years, inspired by your word—your way—
    we have set for ourselves a vision of liberty and justice for all.
    We have heard you whisper to us, even in our darkest moments:
    Live to the vision!

    We confess that over the long years of our history,
    while we have claimed to be your people,
    we have often failed to live to the vision.
    Let us not so fancy the nobility of our vision
    that we fail to remember the times we have neglected
    to claim that vision.

    We confess that too often we have claimed that you were on our side,
    forgetting that you do not choose sides,
    but are always and forever on the side of justice and peace.
    We confess that there have been dark moments in our nation's history,
    as well as bright shining moments
    when we overcame barriers and divisions.
    These we celebrate, and now in these days
    we pray that all that has been given to us might be used to your glory.
    Let us not see the opportunities to show our strength and power,
    forgetting that the truly powerful
    are gracious, generous, humble, forgiving, reconciling.
    Forgive our arrogance, our swagger, our desire
        to see our way as the only way.
    Guard us and guide us to a new strength of purpose,
    to see that all people are recognized as your children
    created in your image,
    entitled to the inalienable rights
    that our country has made its foundation.
    Nourish us in the way of peace, so that all others may be free
    to follow their own pursuit of life and liberty,
    as you steadfastly and surely lead them along their chosen way.

Our grateful songs to you this morning come from hearts aware
that your bounteous goodness is a gift,
your word, our law, your path, our chosen way.
We ask these things in the name of your Son, Jesus Christ,
who brought us true freedom and everlasting peace.
Amen.

A BLESSING

God of Grace and Mercy,
   In the midst of turbulent and mercurial times, we dare to pray!
   We bow before you, the One whose love is from everlasting
   to everlasting,
   whose gift to each and all is life—
   abundant, full, and free.
Whether the market is up or down,
whether our candidate won or lost,
we are reminded that, in God's world, we are one people
called to a future in which peace is possible, poverty challenged,
prejudice unacceptable, and hope the constant companion
of faith-filled people.

In a hungry, hurting, and war-weary world,
we pause to pray for our nation,
whose gateway remains guarded by Lady Liberty,
whose welcome is to the whole world,
whose torch carries the light of liberty and compassion.

So in the sunshine of an historic election,
and in the face of the grim reality of an economic tsunami, we pray:
O God of Eternity, for whom a thousand years is but a day,
we are grateful for this brief moment of borrowed time
in which we live out our lives.
For this moment in history, given to us and to no other,
we ask for grace and wisdom and courage
that we might fashion from the clay of creation
a spirit of generosity.

God of Mercy, we lift up our new leaders.
We pray that you will raise up in them a passion for the good,
so that the values of many may translate into justice for all.
Surround these, your servants, with vision and passion
for a world made new and whole.

We place our times, our nation, our world, and all who lead in your hands,
but we hold out our hands as well,
for in the end, God of Eternity, we all belong to you
and live in service to your will and to your way.

✠

 4

DONA NOBIS PACEM

Reach for the stars
that shine in the night.
Do not be blinded;
walk into the light.
Listen for the message
the star makes bold.
Good tidings. Great joy. Good news. Bright star.
A son is born. A child is ours.
Peace is within our reach.
Lift your eyes to the skies.
Risk stardust on your face.

God of Justice and Grace and Mercy
   You have always called your people to be future pulled, not past
   driven.
   You invite us to be co-creators in a world that is of your making.
   You urge us to risk—even to fail—looking toward a future that is
   beyond our knowing.
      With humility we pray for guidance as we risk setting forth
      our best ideas.
      We do so in full recognition that your future will always
      be marked by your love for the whole of creation.
      You care for every child created in your image.
   With humility we pray for the courage
   to follow your will and your way.
   All who have walked the grounds of the place
   we lovingly call Chautauqua
   are touched by the beauty of this place and
   almost all surprise themselves as they quietly,
   some with embarrassment,
   declare their experiences spiritual.
We pray for a holy passion to claim minds and hearts
as we move toward a future
   where success is measured by the finest in values,
   a future of justice and mercy and love.
Finally we are moved to pray for a kinder future for all who suffer.
Especially we hold in our hearts the people of Haiti
as they face the future armed with faith alone.
   We pray for ourselves that we might never lose our urge to reach out
   beyond our own familiar borders.
   With gratitude and humility we receive the many gifts
   that have been entrusted to our safe keeping.
Teach us, Holy One, to share! Amen.

God of this and every day:

    We come before you expecting a miracle yet fearful
    of what it might be.

    We come in expectation—our spirits soar as the music of faith
    fills the air.

    We come bringing with us burdens and sorrows, joys and hope.

    We come out of our daily realities, busy lives for some,
    lonely lives for others, safety and security for the few, war and
    famine for too many.

    We come for refreshment, renewal, courage, and peace.

    We come to receive the promise you have made,
    that in your love, there will be no more crying, no more dying,
    no more mourning.

        All things will be made new.

God of all the people:

    Your arms are wide enough to embrace the whole world
    and worlds as yet unknown to us.

    Today we pray especially for the women of the world,
    for those who are the carriers and caretakers of life.

    For those who through no fault of their own bear the ravages of war.

    For those who know violence and yet dare to love, to dream, to hope.

    As we are joined this week by women who live in the midst of conflict,
we pray especially for

        Hanan Ashrawi and the Palestinian people,
        Haleh Esfandiari and the Iranian people,
        Galia Golan and the Israeli people,
        Teni Pirri-Simonian, for the Armenian Orthodox Church
        and the Lebanese people,
        Saken Yacoobi and the Afghani women.

    Grant these women strength of body and soul
    that they might continue to speak peace in the midst of conflict,
    that they might dare to dream of a world where mercy and justice
    are a daily reality.

    Grant to us the courage to hear their stories—to absorb their
    struggles and to join them in the heavenly cry for peace.

God of all the nations:

> You speak every language and are at home in every culture and clime.
> Your love knows no boundaries.
> You brook no separations.
> You call us to love one another.
> Grant us the strength and imagination that it might be so.

God of all our secrets:

> You know us well, where we hurt, why we laugh, who we love.
> You know our doubts, our fears, our dreams yet unrealized.
> In the quiet of this very private moment, in this very public space
> enter into our trembling hearts and make us fully thine.
> Open us to every possibility.
> Give us the courage to cry.

God of the whole of our lives:

> Minister especially this day to those whose names are known
> only in our hearts;
>> those who are ill, those who mourn,
>> those for whom reality grows dim,
>> those whose lives are limited by bigotry and poverty,
>> those too fearful to let life be joyful,
>> those who offer love and tender caring.
>
> Amen.

✦

God of Mystery,

All through the ages we your children have sought to understand you. The enormity of your being is beyond our comprehension. Your capacity to love in the face of generations of challenges that would wilt the patience of most every parent astounds and humbles us.

We cannot see you completely but we can see partially in the ageless stories of your people. We glimpse you in the sacred texts that tell your story and set before us heroes and heroines who, like us, are but flawed human beings—yet in these stories we come to know people you love, ordinary people you have called to extraordinary tasks, people who despite their inadequacies have responded to God's call.

Miracles of miracles, your people cannot be contained in any one sacred book more than in another and, oh, my God, there is so much for us to learn if we will but open ourselves to the wideness of your mercy.

We walk among people who are like us and yet unlike us.

We marvel at the variety of your creatures, at the diversity of stories yet to be written.

Loving God,

We pray you will give us the passion and the courage to see beyond the familiar—to delight in our own house of faith—yet be curious enough to explore the rooms where we have never been.

We pray for the community of people all over the world

who seek you in countless and mysterious ways,

who fervently desire to draw near to you,

who place their hope in your steadfast love and abounding mercy,

and who listen for your voice through rituals and symbols that we do not know or understand.

God of Compassion,

We pray for our global community where there are neighbors whose hope grow dim in the torrential rains and winds of war, of hunger and suffering, and of turmoil and corruption.

Wash away the pain and the confusion with the healing waters of compassion, mercy, and justice.

Show us how to truly be their neighbors,

And to allow them to become ours. Open us to ways that we cannot plan

but which you will show us as we make it our intention to bring humanity ever closer together in your reconciling love.

God,

In this extraordinary space

at the start of this extraordinary week,

we pray for the community of our families and friends with whom we share the most intimate moments of our life.

We pray that, as we risk trust and embrace love, through our encounters we might catch a glimpse of your greatness and generosity.

Now we pray for those in our community who are ill; grant them health and well-being. Now for those who have died and those who grieve, we pray for peace; receive them into the communion of saints.

We ask all these things in the name of the one who taught us who is our neighbor,

who showed us the way toward acceptance of others,

and who led us to those who are strangers that we might become brothers and sisters.

⊹

Loving God,

You who comes to us in our crushing sorrows and in our moments of irreverent joy, we come before you week after week secure in your embrace yet fearful of the unknown path before us. We are so small and the problems of the world so incredibly large. Humans that we are we come with our questions—where do we find hope? How do we dare to step out with courage?

We find answers to our burning questions in those events where good prevailed and courage was claimed and determined souls grew in arid untended soul.

God of Peace,

We give thanks that in our life time we have witnessed the fall of the Berlin Wall, the end of apartheid, the power of nonviolence imbedded in Gandhi and Martin Luther King Jr., the declaration that slavery in any form was against the will of God, and the vision of a people made one expressed in the universal declaration of human rights. For those signs and so many not named here we are thankful and we see that your will and your ways have the last word. So, we pray, instill in us the vision to be bold, caring people in our time and place; help us to write a history of justice and freedom and peace.

God of Life,

We pray especially today for our neighbors, India and China, whose own rich and ancient history has given to us beauty and culture and imagination that enrich our lives and stretch our global reach beyond an easy comfortable encounter. The rich diversity of your creation continues to astound us. You have charged us to love our neighbors as ourselves—bless us, O God, with the openness to love beyond our own understanding.

O God of Mystery and Majesty,

We are bold to pray for ourselves. Thank you, God, for making yourself known to us, for loving us enough that we dare to offer love to a world grown weary with war. Thank you for the gift of youth for those who face the future unafraid—their spirits give us joy. Let us live lives worthy of their trust in us. Amen.

Holy God, Spiritual Shepherd,

We pray today to be released from our need to be your exclusive people; we pray that there is the openness to know that you are God of all people, all creation, one shepherd, one flock.

We know that division is neither your will nor your way and yet we persist in fragmenting the flock. We acknowledge that we have wasted time and energy in distinguishing ourselves as different as though you might not notice us if we were just part of the flock. We pray today for unity among all people and we light a candle as we pray for the passion to be part of the reunion of the family of Abraham.

Oh God, hear us.

Spirit of peace, we confess that ancient and intransigent barriers were built between the faithful and reinforced through the ages. Recognizing that our witness for peace is weakened by our carefully nursed and separated paths we dare to pray today that Hagar and Sarah, mothers of Ishmael and Isaac, might kindle a candle that would give light to the nations and bring peace at last to all children of Abraham. We pray today for all caught in conflict, for all who guard the peace, for all who have the power to take us to war.

Oh God, hear us.

God of Love,

We close our time of prayer with prayers for ourselves. We dare to do this because you first loved us, and if we live in your love as we were taught, God, you alone know the wonder of it all. For those who are sick in body, confused in mind, or sad of spirit bring healing, bring peace, and bring joy. We name them now in this moment of silence; for those who laugh and sing and rejoice in life's rich gifts and energizing love, let us catch their joy. For those who have died, who live now in our memories and for all who grieve, give them rest. Sooth the suffering, comfort the grieving, and be with all who are in harm's way.

Finally, as we are all children of Abraham, bring us together. Amen.

✟

Creator God,
    Whose love for us is boundless,
    whose ways are beyond our understanding,
    whose creativity is greater than we can ever imagine,
    we bow before you at this common altar.
    We come in gratefulness and humility, yet with high expectation.
    We lay before you the concern of our hearts.
    We open ourselves to you in full recognition that you already know
        our hidden sorrows, our most extravagant joys,
        our most fervent prayers.

    Bring justice, grant mercy.

Even as we return to the safety, beauty, and security of this place we acknowledge that we are a world in turmoil. We come together with souls stained by wars. We confess that war is always a failure of the spirit. Too often we pray for peace as though that were your business, God, and not our responsibility. Today we light a candle as a sign and symbol of Chautauqua's commitment to be a peacemaker and for us to live as co-creators of a nonviolent world.

    Bring justice, grant mercy.

We are called to be neighbors to those beyond our reach. We pray
for all your people in this wide world and for our global family;
for those children who are born into loveless families,
for all who go to bed hungry,
who suffer from famine or flood or disease,
for all who are poor in things, bless them with life's necessities,
for all who have plenty, make them rich in soul.

    Bring justice, grant mercy.

Finally, God, we pray for ourselves, for the lonely, the fearful, the sick,
    we who stand in need of your grace,
    a sign of hope, a recognition that there is joy in believing.
But our prayers go beyond Chautauqua as we are called
to be neighbors to those beyond our reach.

We pray for all your people in this wide world and
light a candle for our global family:
for those children who are born into loveless families,
for all who go to bed hungry,
who suffer from famine or flood or disease,
for all who are poor in things, bless them with life's necessities,
for all who have plenty, make them rich in soul.

Bring justice, grant mercy.

This day, we offer a corporate prayer for Africa.

You have richly blessed this continent and its people.
Open our eyes to the gifts of Africa,
the beauty of its mountains and rivers,
its history as old as civilization itself,
Africa's sons and daughters, artists, preachers, potters, scientists,
people whose dreams are as precious and expansive as our own.

Open our hearts to the challenges facing the African people.
Move us to share our bounty that we might be
the neighbor we are called to be.
Relieve us of prejudice born of ignorance.
Encourage our hearts that we might be in your service
until all are fed, housed, clothed, and freed.

Finally, God, you who come to us in our great joys,
our crushing sorrows, and in our lives day to day,
in this moment of silence, hear our unspoken prayers
for those we love and even for ourselves,
we who stand in need of your grace.
Amen.

Loving God,
    We come before you busy about many things,
    heavy with anxiety about those nearest and dearest to us,
    yet beyond our own knowing the needs and
    burdens we carry that you already hold.
God of our hearts,
    Forgive us for fearing we cannot do it all
    still our fluttering with the assurance that we are your children,
    loved and blessed beyond our doing.
We confess that we grow weary of the reality that daily confronts us:
    Your children who wander homeless
    the hungry who cry for bread
    the captives who long for freedom,
    violence and the seeming endless grief of those who mourn.
Great and good God,
    We praise your deep compassion but we are not God
    and we have our hands full.
    Help us to hear your call to justice and to loving service.
    Free us from the paralysis of guilt and
    show us the peace that flows from loving deeds, the surprising
    strength that compassion instills in us.
    Forgive us our fears and remind us that love,
    freely given, is the greatest gift we can give to you, God,
    to ourselves, and to others.
    Stir us to ardent service, your abundant life to share.
In humility, we pray, lead us to do those good and true things
    that bear witness to a generosity of spirit that your love for us
    has made possible.
    As much as can be, spirit God, fall afresh on us—mend us, fill us,
    and make us bloom.
    Amen.

✠

Holy God

You created for us a large and beautiful world; you promised us a world-house with many mansions where you would be with us for all eternity.

We confess that sometimes we are overwhelmed by the possibilities and diversity in your expansive world and we try to downsize the dream . . . to scale it to our finite capacity.

From the beginning as the world was formed there were contrasts and complements, night and day, sun and moon, work and rest, male and female, and you declared it all to be good! We try to wrap our arms around your gift of love and unity and wholeness. But we confess that too often we violate your vision of unity and create in our own small world; we fragment and divide. We build walls, you tear them down, and we create artificial boundaries and call them nation states, and we fail to see the world through the eyes of faith, a world without walls, a world with shared oceans and sky, moon, and stars. Forgive us, reform us, and make us whole.

Holy God

We are surrounded by the beauty of nature. We walk more lightly on these grounds, our eyes pulled upward by the bluest of skies, shaded by ancient trees that form a canopy of green. We are surrounded by a symphony of sound: birds and creature of many names, the lilting voices of tiny children, the soothing lullabies of loving parents. We confess that we are tempted to want this world for only our own and yet we know that the gifts that we have received are to be shared that they might transform a world weary with poverty and bigotry and war. May this place of beauty that bears witness to your generosity and boundless imagination be for us an inspiration to be your whole people. We make our confession in the sure knowledge that . . .

> *In compassion God forgives us;*
> *Enable us to turn from the way of violence and division.*
> *Show us how to choose and cherish life.*

Amen.

✠

Forgiving God,
>Let us confess the secret sins in the hidden spaces of our lives
>which hold us in fear and anguish, keeping us from God
>and one another.
>Let us confess the allure of the kingdoms of this world
>that seduce us with the guarantees of security, comfort,
>predictability, youth, beauty, longevity.
>Kingdoms that promise plenty, promises that crowd out the
>possibility of peace,
>Peace that is within reach and yet beyond our understanding.
>Peace that requires struggles, courage, and faith.
>They crowd out the peace that disrupts what is and grants
>a quiet satisfaction that is beyond our understanding.

Let us confess
>The words of judgment we have spoken too freely in our cities,
>our nation, our places of work, even places of worship.
>The compromises we have made that allow evil to multiply,
>producing harvests of destruction and death.

Let us confess
>the complacency with which we live,
>the ease with which we keep our prejudices,
>refusing to be the one people for which Jesus prayed.

Let us confess
>the seduction of war and the allure of victory,
>the roll of the drums, the drama of bombs bursting in air.

Prince of Peace,
>Stir our hearts, make us bold to follow your will, your ways.
>God from whom nothing is hidden,
>you know the motives of our hearts.
>Forgive us our sins and declare to us the joyful truth,
>that we are a loved and liberated people.

✠

God of all creation,
> We are surrounded by beauty and majesty,
> old, old trees that heard the words of Vincent and Miller,
> Susan B. Anthony, Booker T. Washington,
> the Reverend Anna Howard Shaw, Franklin Delano Roosevelt,
> old, old trees that hold sacred our secrets,
> old, old trees that have withstood many a storm and been blessed by
> the certainty of every day's rising of the sun,
> old, old trees whose leaves grant shade and filter the sun.
> All these are your gifts to your people. You whose eye
> is on the sparrow, surely you watch over us.
> Forgive us for taking so much for granted, for doubting that you
> care for us and provide for our needs, for worrying too much
> about tomorrow.

God of justice,
> You have created all people in your image;
> you treasure every newborn child, whether born to king or beggar,
> princess or prostitute.
> You weep when new life is neither nurtured nor treasured,
> when babies, through no fault of their own, are received
> as a burden, not a blessing.
> Today your tears are shed for Africa's children caught
> in a web of war and famine and disease.
> We confess to turning away from this distant disaster too remote
> to comprehend too much the stranger to call family.
> We confess to our failure to cradle these children born too far away
> to hold close. We are grateful for those who call us to account but
> confess too often their cares become a substitute for our own.

God of grace and glory,
> Strength for today brought hope for tomorrow.
> We have every reason to be your faithful people,
> yet we allow our plenty to mask our need for your grace
> We make happiness our goal when down deep we know that hope is
> born of struggles overcome and love runs deepest in our darkest hour.

We confess that our faith sometimes comes too easily and acknowledge that faith under fire instructs us, tempers us, and bears witness to others.
Forgive us for striving last for the dominion of God, putting instead our energy into treasures on earth.

✠

God of grace, love, and compassion,
> We confess that we have failed to love you
> with our whole heart and soul and mind.
> Forgive us our foolish ways.

God of creation,
> You formed us in your image.
> We confess that all too often we recreate you
>> in our image.
> We confess that we limit our love and reach out
>> only to those who look like us.
> Forgive us our ways.

God of this world and worlds yet unknown,
> We confess that we name as neighbor
>> only those whose world we know and understand.
> Forgive us our failure to name each of your creatures
> "neighbor,"
> for each is a rare treasure to be loved and protected.
> Forgive us our foolish ways.

O God who alone can probe the depths of our hearts,
> Hear the prayer of the humble and justify the repentant sinner.
> Grant us the gift of a heart that beats
>> beyond boundaries
>>> and loves without limits.

✛

 **5**

GRANT US COURAGE
FOR THE LIVING OF THESE DAYS

Precious Lord, take our hands. Lead us on.
Claim us for the ministry of justice.
Heal the wounded and wipe the tears of all who suffer.
Help us to be to one another a blessing. Amen.

Creator God
> We see you in the rainbow where the storm and the sunlight meet
> and we receive with grateful hearts your promised covenant.
> You have given to us a world to be treasured and preserved—
> people to be fed, clothed, housed, and freed,
> a world of peace and love and justice.

Good Shepherd, you promise us no one will be lost.
> Your promises hold: they are true and can be trusted.
> But in this beautiful sunlit morning it is not your promises, O God,
> that create our uneasiness, it is our response.
> You created us as people with free will—with the capacity to make
> choices.
> We make our choices and it is those choices
>> combined with the choices of others
>> that define the world in which your children live.

Today we pray for wisdom and for generosity of spirit.
> Guide us to embrace a sense of life rooted in a reality beyond
> ourselves.
> Stir in us a passion for justice.
> Help us to know and understand that our choices matter,
> that those who are hungry and hurting and terrified call to us
> and our response to their calls, their pain, will make us whole.
> Here we will find inspiration for the truly moral life.

Generous God
> Our instinct too often is to separate ourselves
> from those we do not understand.
> We built walls of division and create misunderstanding.
> We pray for the courage to tear down those walls,
> for the imagination to see in all people, of every faith or no faith,
> a partner for peace.

How great is your love, Lord God, how wide is your mercy!
> Never let us board up the wide gate that leads to life
> with narrow rules or doctrines that you dismiss;
> But give us a Spirit to welcome all people with affection,
> so that your church may never exclude secret friends of yours,
> who are included in the love of Christ, who came to save us all.

We pray for young people whose lives are before them,
who dare to dream of a world of promise and peace.
Be with them in their yet unwritten journey.
We pray today for those whose hearts are heavy
with the loss of their loved ones.
We pray for those who have died. In doing so they live in our memory.
We pray as well for those whose names we do now call
but you are yet their shepherd.
Healing God, we pray for all who are lost and lonely,
those who have given up on life.
Renew their spirit.
We pray as well for those whose lives are compromised by illness
and for those who care for them.
We have opened ourselves to you.
You reach out to us and timidly we reach for your embrace.
We know you care for us and so we pray now
for those whose choices are limited
by illness, by sadness, by grief, by physical limitation,
by anxiety, by poverty, by prejudice.
Grant them well-being and peace of mind and heart
and if it be your will, make of us a miracle in their lives.
And where storm and sunlight meet,
may thy kingdom come on earth as it is in heaven.
Amen.

✛

Creator God,

> You placed a song in Mary's heart and, miraculously, the word in her womb was the same as the word on her lips. We give thanks for Mary's courage, for Mary's openness to God's words of justice and peace, and for all the Marys in this day and in days gone by who have risked the pain and uncertainty of giving life. We pray especially for those who must give birth in unwelcoming, unsafe, unkempt places. We pray for the day when every baby's first cry is a cause for rejoicing.

Loving God,

> You saw Mary as a woman of faith and placed in her womb the one who would become for us our rock and our salvation. We pray today for all the Marys who have kept the faith alive when the forces of darkness would have extinguished the light. For women who preach and teach and pray, for women who sing and paint and create, for mothers who pass on faith's lessons of hope and promises to their children. For the women who have broken the barriers erected to keep their talents hidden and limited and for the men who have joined them in this struggle, we say a grateful "Amen." For Joan Chittester and Jean Zarou, the women of Neva Shalom, peacemakers all and so many more, we give thanks.

Holy God,

> You chose Mary to be the messenger for your word of justice, to be among the first to announce the hope of resurrection, and we remember all the Marys who have, through the ages, risked speaking truth to power. Grant voice to women today who make peace at the risk of their very lives, and open our ears, O God, to hear their words of forgiveness and reconciliation.

Embracing God,

> You gave Mary strength for the struggle you knew would be hers, and so today we honor all the Marys for whom life is a struggle. You blessed women with beauty and crafted them as vessels of love. Yet too many have been violated and misused. Their bodies have been broken and their light has been extinguished. We pray for all the world's women whose talents have not been nourished, who have been robbed of their youth and promise. Forgive and redeem those who failed to care for God's creations.

Finally, God, you come to us in our most irreverent moments
of joy and in our deepest sorrow.

> We rejoice in the name of Mary, the brave one, the just Mary, the
> suffering one, Mary the valiant, Mary whose life blessed the
> feminine in all of us, so in Mary's caring name, we pray for all who
> have died and those who grieve that loss. We pray as well for those
> whose life is burdened with illness and pain. Grant health, and if
> that is not to be, bring peace at last. Open all hearts to receive
> Mary's word of resurrection.

✠

Holy God,
  Holy Immortal One,
May this time in worship
  grant to us
    strength for life's journey,
    courage for the times of suffering,
    the power of forgiveness,
    the joy of faith,
    the freedom of love,
    the hope of new life,
    the vision of unity.
May this time in worship
  open us to the call to serve.

✠

Almighty and most gracious God,
You, by your very nature, are present in good times and in bad;
    in warm days and in cold;
    in wind, rain, and sunny life;
    in laughter and in pain;
    in joy and in despair;
    in work and in play;
    and in all those things that are a joy of life.
Today, in newborn trust, we pray,
    turn back, O God, the outer layers of our selves,
    and look beneath the surface to our hidden inner depths.
    Many of us hide behind polite dreams and wooden responses,
    not daring to admit to others or even to ourselves
    that we are vulnerable.
    Yet we turn to you, trusting,
    knowing that you will handle us carefully and tenderly.
    Turn back the outer layers of apparent courage,
    and find our fears.
    Address them in us.
Precious Lord, you know us as we are.
    We confess to you, Lord, what we are:
    We are not the people we like others to think we are;
    we are afraid to admit even to ourselves what lies in the depths of
    our souls.
    But we do not want to hide our true selves from you.
    We believe that you know us as we are and yet you love us.
    Help us not to shrink from self-knowledge:
    Teach us to respect ourselves for your sake;
    give us the courage to put our trust in your guiding power.
    Raise us out of the paralysis of guilt
        into the freedom and energy of forgiven people.
For those who through long habit
    find forgiveness hard to accept,
    we ask you to break their bondage and set them free.
    We ask not that you make the hard moments easier,
    except that our burdens are

eased by the assurance of your companionship,
heightened by the knowledge of your loving care,
strengthened by hope,
and shaped by love.
Through Jesus Christ our Lord.
Amen.

Note: Adapted from the United Church of Christ Book of Worship.

✠

Merciful God
We come this morning as humble people
 awed by the world in which
 we live and move and have our being.
 Solid concrete bridges fall,
 wars rage, loving relationships shatter, babies cry,
 we turn away from your people for absurd reasons of our own making.
 Children laugh and play, lovers rejoice.
 Risks are taken—justice breaks out, peace remains possible.
 So we come to this place to seek guidance for the living or our days.
You breathed life into us, trusted us, and set us free
 to make our own choices,
 to map our spiritual DNA.
 We would rather not bear the responsibility.
 We confess our confusions, our timidity, our fears.
 Guide us, gracious God, into a life that sides with truth,
 that rejoices in justice.
 Teach us to be co-creators with you of a world
 where a new baby's cry is an announcement that
 your holy order of justice and love and peace will prevail.
Keep watch over and forgive us all our sins and remind us
we are all both flawed and loved.
In spite of our tendency to pull apart, in spite of our tenacity
to our old ways,
Loving God, you continue to call us back together again,
showing us the true nature of forgiveness and reconciliation.
God stands within the shadow, keeping watch about God's own. Amen.

✜

Almighty God,
We come to you today confessing that
we are not the people we like others to think we are.
We are afraid to admit even to ourselves
what lies in the depths of our souls.
But we do not want to hide our true selves from you.
We believe that you know us as we are,
and yet you love us.
Help us not to shrink from self-knowledge.
Teach us to respect ourselves, not for our sake but for your sake.
Give us the courage to put our trust in your guiding power.
Raise us out of the paralysis of guilt
into the freedom and energy of a forgiven people.
And for those who through long habit find forgiveness hard to accept,
we ask you to break this bondage and set them free.

✛

CALL TO WORSHIP[10]

Sisters and Brothers;
We are not alone.
We live in God's world.
We believe in God,
who has created and is creating,
who calls us to reconcile and make new.
We trust God,
who calls us to be the church,
to love and serve others,
to seek justice,
to live with love and mercy
to proclaim the good news.
In life, in death, in life, beyond death,
God is with us.
We are not alone.
Thanks be to God.

✟

---

10. Originally written for the World Council of Churches circa 1990.

God of Justice and Compassion

We come before you today mindful of our history as a nation. We recall with sorrow and sadness the sins of our dark past; we remember those who lived burdened with the pain of slavery. We are in awe of their unbelievable capacity for faith in the face of undeserved suffering. We are humbled by their slave songs filled with hope and with the belief that the rising of every sun carried the promise of a new day, so for those whose ancestors were slaves and to freedom fighters alike, we give thanks. They teach us the meaning of faith for our time.

> *Lift every voice and sing, till earth and heaven ring,*
> *ring with the harmonies of liberty;*
> *let our rejoicing rise, high as the listening skies,*
> *let it resound loud as the rolling sea.*

We acknowledge today that we come to the freedoms we enjoy over a way that by tears have been watered. We come to a place where our people sighed and we acknowledge that the suffering goes on. Good great God, your children still weep and your love calls us each and every one to give our best for justice everywhere. We pray with heavy hearts for the courage to stand where the white gleam of our bright star is cast; keep us forever in the right path we pray.

> *Lift every voice and sing, till earth and heaven ring,*
> *ring with the harmonies of liberty;*
> *let our rejoicing rise, high as the listening skies,*
> *let it resound loud as the rolling sea.*

"God of our weary years, God of our silent tears," we stand before you humbled by humanities' capacity for cruelty and for your continued love for us; you lead us into the light and point the way to love and liberty.

God of all people—of all that is or ever has been, lest we forget you, we open our hearts and our minds to your lessons of love and redemption and courage. Today we remember our past and, as we face the rising sun of a new day beginning, we commit ourselves to your will for all your children. We pray, let us live the life of faith that the dark past has taught us. So we lift our voices and sing.

Sing "Lift Every Voice and Sing."[11]

---

11. "Lift Every Voice and Sing," words by James Weldon Johnson, 1921; tune, Lift Every Voice, J. (John) Rosamond Johnson, 1921, © 1921 Edward B. Marks. Music Co.

Gracious God
>Long before our memories were formed
>you were guiding your children toward justice and mercy.
>They like we resisted the path illumined by your great love,
>and war and famine and bigotry and bitterness came to be.
>Down through endless ages your people
>have confessed their failure to live as those who have received
>the gift of your astonishing forgiving love for us.
>And so we claim, claim anew

Great is thy faithfulness!

Holy God Immortal One
>We sing and pray and pronounce that you are our God
>and we are your people.
>We recite and acknowledge that we are commanded
>to love no other God.
>Forgive us for hearing these words as an order, not a grace.
>You have freed us to be mere mortals
>on a journey with our God.
>Forgive our failure to be grateful for our limits
>and to rejoice in the mercy you grant us each morning.
>And so we claim anew

Great is thy faithfulness!

Faithful God
>We confess we need you.
>You come among us and sit beside us
>and hear us speak and see us ignore you
>and heal our pain and let us wound you.
>You love us to the end
>and triumph over all our hatred.
>We confess we need you, God,
>and so we sing with joy.

(Sing the hymn "Great Is Thy Faithfulness."[12])

---

12. "Great Is Thy Faithfulness," tune, Faithfulness, William Runyon, 1923.

Gracious Lord,
> We come into your presence
> a worried people;
> so much seems suddenly so uncertain.
> We pray thy will be done
> but we confess we'd like to give you a little advice;
> we acknowledge that we are wedded to our own ways
> yet something stirs inside of us and
> we sing of your amazing love
> yet we find it frightening,
> daunting,
> demanding;
> "Love so amazing, so divine."

>> *Love so amazing, so divine,*
>> *Demands my life, my soul, my all.*

Holy God
> We confess that we measure the worth of others,
> and sometimes even our own worth,
> by our financial well-being.
> We know better.
> We know that life itself is your greatest gift to us and
> that you grant us the gift of years and
> call us to live in service to others.
> We know that you will always receive us.
> So fearfully we put ourselves in your hands and
> give back to you the time you have gifted to us.
> We confess that we are hesitant
> to accept your freely given love,
> yet we dare to open ourselves to love so amazing.

(Sing "When I Survey the Wondrous Cross."[13])

✛

---

13. "When I Survey the Wondrous Cross," words by Isaac Watts, 1707; tune, anon.

Holy God, Holy and Mighty One, Holy Immortal One,
have mercy upon us, Holy God,

> We are your children and, oh, how we yearn to walk in your way.
> But we find ourselves lost in a morass of worry and ambition and plans
> of our own that leave no room for the way you have set before us.
> The joy you offer to us on the way eludes us and we confess that we
> are in our own way and ask you to set us on the path that leads to life.

Holy and Mighty One,

> Your power is beyond our understanding. Your kingdom is a vision
> of justice and dignity and peace.
> Sadly our ways are not your ways. You bless the poor, you feed the
> hungry with good things and on a starlit night you birthed a life-
> giving savior.
> You offer us hope and healing in a world weary with war and
> poverty. We confess that we too often fail to reach out to touch you.

We confess that we need you, God. Heal us and make us whole.

Christe, eleison; Christe eleison; Christe, eleison.

Holy Immortal One,

> You give to us, your wayward flock, the greatest gift of all—
> life (abundant full and free).
> Forgive us our failure to be grateful—our always wanting more.
> No, we don't get to stay forever but what we do with the life
> you give us is the gift we give to you so, Holy One, Mighty and
> Immortal One, teach us to love as we live and forgive us
> when we confuse our mortality with your immortality.

You are our God and we are your people.

Kyrie, eleison; Kyrie, eleison; Kyrie, eleison

Holy God, source of joy, we receive the blessing of your forgiveness
and are comforted by your promise that the past is over and gone,
and all things are made new. Amen.

✢

PRAYER BASED ON PSALM 27

We confess, gracious God,
    that we are not worthy of your love for us,
    that we fear and stumble,
    when we have a mighty stronghold within us,
    that we fear to act because we think we are small,
    when the greatness of your power lies within our reach.
O God, forgive our blindness and helplessness.
    We look, but do not see.
    The armies of hate and injustice are encamped against us.
    Make us bold and mighty ambassadors of your justice.
    Where there is anger, help us to see love.
    Where there is ugliness, help us to see beauty.
    When we see curves and detours in the path ahead,
    help us to see your straight path.
Teach us your ways,
    so we may bask in your Truth.
    Teach us your love,
    so there may be light in the land,
        through the grace of our Lord,
            who strengthens forever. Amen.

✠

Gracious God,
We confess what seems to be always with us:
Broken things within us that seem never to mend,
empty places within us that seem always to ache,
things like buds within us that seem never to flower.
O God of love and grace,
help us accept ourselves;
>   we confess to you, Lord, what we are:
>   We are not the people we like others to think we are;
>   we are afraid to admit even to ourselves
>   what lies in the depths of our souls.
>   But we do not want to hide our true selves from you.
>   We believe that you know us as we are, and yet you love us.
Help us not to shrink from self-knowledge:
>   Teach us to respect ourselves for your sake.
It is in loving ourselves that we are ennobled to love our neighbor.
It is in accepting our shortcomings that we are open to forgiving others.
It is in accepting our imperfections that we are saved from needing
>   to be perfect.
And so in humility we pray,
>   lead us to do those good and true things
>   that bear witness to a generosity of spirit
>   that your love for us has made possible.
As much as can be, spirit God, fall afresh on us.
>   Mend us, fill us, and make us bloom.
>   Give us the courage to put our trust in your guiding power.
>   Amen.

Note: Adapted from the United Church of Christ Book of Prayer.

✠

 6

TAKE MY HAND, PRECIOUS LORD

Loving God,
Take our wondering, our worrying, and our wandering
    and weave it into something strong.
Take our differences, our suspicions, and our tightly held perceptions
    and help us to see common wisdom.
Weave the strands of our diverse personalities and beliefs
    into a tapestry made beautiful by virtue of its multitextured threads.
You are our God and we are your people.
Feed us with things of the spirit.

Open our eyes to a vision of the future that is bold and brave
    and worthy of the gifts we have been given.
We are called to be hopeful people who believe
    that every darkness is broken by the dawning of a new day,
every death is marked by the cry of a newborn babe,
    and hopeless illnesses sometimes,
    in shaa Allah, God willing,
    are miraculously healed and new possibilities come forth.
    Amen.

✠

CALL TO WORSHIP

We are not alone.
We live in God's world.
We are not afraid.
We receive God's promises.
We are not timid.
We are borne up on eagles' wings
and held in the palm of God's hand.
We are not anxious about our lives.
We are God's little flock,
to whom God gives the kingdom.
In life, in death,
in life beyond death,
God is with us.
We are not alone.

✠

Holy God,

In the quiet of this place, having confessed in song that you are precious . . . Lord, we risk saying aloud that we need you. So, daring to be vulnerable, we reach out and we pray, take my hand . . . lead us in these uncertain times.

Things that were certain just a short time ago elude us and anxiety creeps into our secure plans. Suddenly the future is not ours alone to claim. Young people discover that jobs are hard to find and too many worry that health will fail and resources will be inadequate. Retirement seems more distant, less assured. Decisions require more discernment—we stand in need of prayer.

We could so easily be burdened with fear or despair, but we are God's people and God does not desert us, but calls us to be community for one another . . . families reach out beyond their own and caring expands to meet our needs.

So, there is hope and faith and love, Holy One. Guide my feet— take my hand.

You are precious, Lord. We rest easy in your hand.

Amen.

✛

Merciful God,
　You created us in your image.
　Like every artist, you stepped back from the work
　of your hands and called it good.
　Forgive us when we fail to see your hand in our own lives
　and in the lives of neighbors near and far.
　Your signature was affixed in our DNA,
　each creature special, each one crafted for a purpose.
　Forgive us when we go our own way,
　mindful only of our desires, failing to seek your purpose.
Merciful God,
　We know that you love us and that you call us to fullness of life.
　Forgive us our reluctance when the call comes in burning bushes
　and in still, small voices.
　Why is it that your call comes, expectant God,
　at the very moment in which we plead inadequacy?
　In the face of your clear call,
　like those who went before us,
　we plead that we are ordinary.
　Forgive us for failing to comprehend
　the extraordinary tasks for which we have been equipped.
　Forgive us our timidity in the face of today's challenges.
　Forgive us and whisper again to our fainting hearts,
　be of good courage.
　A hungry, hurting, war weary world has need of your
　　　　Courage . . . Courage . . . Courage.
　Amen.

✠

Precious Lord,
  Your holy Word tells us not to worry,
  not about our life or our bodies or what tomorrow may bring.
  Sadly, we confess that we are a worrying people and
  trusting totally in your care for us is just too hard to accept.
  We are your children and we yearn to walk in your way.
  But we find ourselves lost in a morass of worry and ambition and
  plans of our own that leave no room for the way you have set before us.

  You offer joy to us yet the way eludes us and
  we confess that often we are in our own way and
  ask you to set us on the path that leads to life.
  You tell us that worrying cannot add a single hour
  to our span of life and
  that your vision for us is a life that is full and free.
  With humility we confess that we too often fail to depend
  on your immortal love—
  open us to the gift of your love that even death can never destroy.
  Take from our souls the strain and strife and
    let our ordered lives confess the liberation of your grace.
      Amen.

Loving God,
There is fear in the land and we find ourselves anxious about a host
of unknowns. We confess that we approach the future as though
everything depends on our planning, our insights, and our capacity
to prepare for all circumstances. Yet we know you are a God of
surprises and if we will but let you into the hidden recesses of our
minds, where anxiety lives, then we will say with the psalmist of old:

The Lord is the stronghold of my life; of whom,
of what shall I be afraid? (Psa. 27:1)

We are an impatient people. We confess that our ready access to
material comfort shields us from a world of want, where heartfelt
desires, even life's essentials, are in short supply for too many of
your people. We confess that our abundance is both a gift and a
challenge and we say with the psalmist of old, "Teach us your way, O
God." Teach us patience; open us to the lessons learned from those
for whom the words of the psalmists are the Bread of Life. Hear
anew these words of comfort:

I believe that I shall see the goodness of the Lord
in the land of the living. (Psa. 27:13)

Wait for the Lord, says the psalmist. Now in this quiet moment we
confess that waiting on a God we cannot see nor touch nor taste nor
hear is not easy for a people blessed with great gifts, people who can
create for themselves a secure future.

And still we know that we are vulnerable mortal beings.
We disappoint ourselves and confess that the future we create
is often neither wise nor truly secure.

So we confess once again that the ancient words of the psalmist
minister to our needs that are too deep for us to speak, too
frightening for us to face. Hear again the biblical wisdom:

Hope in God and take heart. Hope in the Lord. (Psa. 27:14)

✛

God of the ages and architect of a future yet to be revealed,

You have been our help in ages past and hope for years to come. Yet we confess that our anxieties grow, our fears unsettle us and we fail to acknowledge that only in your love are we sheltered from the stormy blast.

From everlasting you are God, to endless years the same. We hear these words and wrestle with the enormity of their meaning. Why is it, O God, that we so firmly believe that our defenses against an uncertain world are in our hands alone? Forgive us for our failure to receive your love, to rest easy in the knowledge that sufficient is your arm alone and only in the shadow of your throne will we dwell secure.

Grant to us the peace that can come when we acknowledge that only your defense is sure.

Gracious God, we affirm with hope your presence in the world. We confess that when trouble comes we fret and fuss and blame and deny. We close doors and turn away good help when all we would have to do is ask. We forget that time will bear us all away. Forgive us and be thou our guide while troubles last, and our eternal home.

✛

Healing God,
We come before you believing
and yet filled with doubt.
Forgive us our failure to trust your ability
to relieve our anxiety.
We bow before you beset with demons that tempt us.
We are the people of too much:
Too much food,
too much wealth,
too much knowledge,
too little understanding,
too much information,
too little truth,
too many choices,
too little time.
Break us loose from these bonds
and lead us into a responsive life
where all our bounty is gratefully shared.
In the quiet of this worship,
we approach your throne of grace,
unworthy tempted sinners, each and every one,
none so pure, none so perfect
that we have no need of your peace.

✛

 7

BEHOLD,
I MAKE ALL THINGS NEW—
REVELATION 21:5

Healing and Holy God,
We your children are here again in your presence
professing that we are weary with confessing,
hoping that we might hide our sins
from your all encompassing presence.
Knowing this is not possible,
we do pray that you, who sees all,

know that we try to be our best selves.
Still we confess that at times
we find ourselves hard to love
even as you assure us that you love
our most unlovely selves.

Despite our weakness, you surprise us with abundant blessings
and out of our weakness we find the strength to love.
Open our hearts that we might make room
for your gift of forgiveness.
Release us from the paralysis of guilt into the
freedom and energy of forgiven people.
For those of us who find forgiveness hard to accept,
we ask you to break us out of our bondage
and set us free.
Amen.

✛

Eternal God,

    Your look is long, your vision focused, forever forward,
    your surprises few.
    Your hope holds even in desperate times,
    your passion forever for the vulnerable,
    your forgiveness always available,
    your love beyond our comprehension.

You are our God and we are your people.

    We come, worried, uncertain, humbled by our circumstances,
    saddened by the suffering of so many:
    The jobless, the lonely, the elderly.
    We look anew to our faith to sustain us
    and hopefully to maintain us,
    as we are generous people whose hope is rooted, not in success,
    but in our capacity for compassion.
    We remain the fortunate ones of our world.
    Help us to realize that our good fortune is not entirely
    of our own making,
    rather it is rooted in blessing bestowed upon us.

We pray,

    teach us longevity, the staying power of love,
    the comfort of the compassionate, the humility of limits.
    The imagination needed for survival in tough times.
    Help us to discern the truly important,
    the majesty of challenge, the faith inherent in risk.

Please, God, keep us safe. We know we ask too much but

    we ask it for all your children everywhere,
    for our President and his impossible calling,
    and, yes, for Chautauqua and the spirit it brings to us all. Amen.

Merciful God,

    You are a kind and generous God.
    Out of your love for us you sent your only Son to bring to earth,
    your message of unity and peace and justice,
    to give sight to the blind, release to the captives, food to the hungry,
    courage to all who dare to follow your way.
    Your love gives life, not death, the last word.

Holy God,
> You weep when your people suffer.
> You forgive when we fail to forgive one another.
> You offer peace in angel songs
> and we are too often deaf to the message.
> War breaks out and lives are lost and love is shattered.
> Yet your love for us is eternal,
> your healing powers readily available to all
> who have the courage to pray, "Your will, not mine, be done."

In the quiet of this moment,
> we pray for your healing touch.
> We pray for healing between warring nations.
> We pray for healing within our nation.
> We pray that the spirit of peace might move mightily
> across this world.
> We pray for an end to voices that lead us to hate and hurt.

Good and gracious God,
> Open us to the possibility that generosity of spirit just might be
> stronger than winning battles that never needed to be fought.
>> We pray for all of us that we might look in each other's eyes
>> and see the face of God.

We pray for people of faith that all division might be healed,
>> That our witness might be marked by compassion
>> so that the world might believe.
> We pray that we might break down age-old barriers
>> and come at last to one common altar
>> where we might receive together the gifts of God
>> for the people of God.
> We pray especially this week for all who are in pain,
>> and for all who face unknown illness,
>> all who await the doctor's healing touch.
> We pray for doctors, nurses, hospitals, midwives, healers all.
> We pray for all who grieve any loss of love or life,
> and new life and love enriched by treasured memories.
> Our most heartfelt prayers are for those who grieve from misplaced
> words of hate or anger,

for distances between parents and children,
    for love offered and not received.
We pray for all who give love to all others,
for children whose happy faces make us smile,
for husbands and wives, for years of tenderness,
for lovers and partners and friends, for pastors, teachers, and healers,
for those who would heal a mean spirited community.
Grant them courage that they might stand strong in the face of harm,
    that they by their witness might overcome all efforts to hurt or destroy.
We pray, merciful God, that love might have its way,
        that we open ourselves to the possibility that your healing power
        might bring us the peace we seek. Amen.

Loving and forgiving God, Spirit Divine,
> We come before you to confess what you already know.
> Secret sins in the hidden spaces of our lives,
> sins you have already forgiven.
> Mistakes we cannot forget, that keep you, O God, out of our lives.
> Burdens that keep us from loving each other.
> Forgive us for our failure to accept your boundless love for us.
> Open our eyes, Spirit Divine, to your will for us,
> to a life full and free:

> *Silently now I wait for thee,*
> *ready, my God, thy will to see.*
> *Open my eyes, illumine me, Spirit divine!*

Spirit of truth,
> We confess that we sometimes feel overwhelmed
> by the reality of the world's suffering.
> It is too much to bear!
> The cries of the poor are too painful to hear.
> We feel helpless.
> Burdened with the concerns of our own lives,
> we lose the opportunity to receive the healing balm
> of a compassionate life.
> Open our ears that we might hear as we listen
> and respond with love.

> *Silently now I wait for thee,*
> *ready, my God, thy will to see.*
> *Open my eyes, illumine me, Spirit divine!*

Spirit Divine, Holy One,
> Giver of birth and rebirth,
> we confess that we resist the coming of the spirit
> into our well-planned lives.
> We confess that our carefully constructed religious rules
> can be barriers to the life of faith.
> Open our hearts to the disruption of your presence.

Surprise us with your love,
and grant to us the courage to receive your blessing.

> *Silently now I wait for thee,*
> *ready, my God, thy will to see.*
> *Open my eyes, illumine me, Spirit divine!*[14]

✛

---

14. "Open My Eyes, That I May See," words and music by Clara Scott, 1895;
tune Open My Eyes.

Almighty and merciful God,
we have erred and strayed from your way like lost sheep.

    We have followed too much the devices and desires of our own hearts.

    We have offended against your holy laws.

    We have left undone those things we ought to have done.

    Our to-do lists fail to include reminders to love,

    to forgive, and to forget,

    to be extravagant in our giving,

    to be understanding especially of those whose ways are not our ways.

Merciful God,

    We have done those things we ought not to have done.

    We have kept score of our generosity and

    recorded the failure of others to do likewise.

    We have closed our eyes to the cry of the needy

    and we tell ourselves they are not worthy.

    We have confused our ways with your ways

    and imposed our will on others;

    we have placed our faith in false gods and have failed to

    commit our souls into your hands.

        O Lord, have mercy upon us.

✛

PRAYER FOR THE END OF THE CHAUTAUQUA SEASON

Now as we part, let our memories of this season be of peace.
Let us set aside all animosities that plague us
and prejudices that divide us.
And, for the sake of our children and grandchildren,
let us offer now to one another the sign of peace.
We do this not as a simple gesture of friendship,
but as a sign that we wish to be at peace with all people.
We look into the face of a stranger,
and there we see the face of God.
Let us join in this act of reconciliation
and prayerfully greet one another
with the ancient words said round the world:
    "The peace of God be with you,"
and respond, "And also with you."

✠

❊ 8 ❊

NOW ABIDE FAITH/HOPE/LOVE— THE GREATEST OF THESE IS LOVE— CORINTHIANS 13

Nothing that is worth doing can be achieved in our lifetime;
therefore we must be saved by hope.
Nothing which is true or beautiful or good makes complete sense
in any immediate context of history;
therefore we must be saved by faith.
Nothing we do, however virtuous, can be accomplished alone;
therefore we must be saved by love.[15]

---

15. Reinhold Neibuhr, *The Irony of American History* (Chicago: University of Chicago Press, 1952), 63.

Holy God,
Holy Immortal One,
Grant us forgiveness.
Transform our desire for peace
    into sure and certain acts of courage.
May the God of love who shared his love
    strengthen us in our love for one another.
May the Son who shared his life
    grant us grace that we might share our lives,
and may the Holy Spirit dwelling in us
    empower us to be only and always
        for others.
        Go in peace.
God of Mystery and Majesty,
    We come to you uncertain
    and challenged by the times in which we live.
    We find ourselves seeking solutions to problems we thought
    we had already resolved.
    We acknowledge the shaking of the foundations of our lives
    and even of our treasured institutions.
    We confess that we thought we were the good planners
    and that the future was in our hands.
    We come humbled by our unknowing,
    Unsure we are open in new ways to the future
    you have in store for your people.
    Newly needy, we pray that our eyes might be opened
    and our hearts stirred by the lessons of loss.
    Turn our worries into compassion and our anxieties
    into centering prayer.
    Forgive us for forgetting that your future is for all your children,
    a mystery beyond our imagining.
    Forgive our failure, God, to find security and comfort
    in the wisdom of the ages.
    Amen.

✠

Holy God,
　　Whose ways are not our ways
　　and whose thoughts are not our thoughts,
　　grant that your Holy Spirit may intercede for us
　　with sighs too deep for words.
　　Heal our wounded hearts
　　where they are made heavy by sorrow.
　　We pray for all those in this community
　　whose loss of loved ones
　　still brings tears to the eye
　　and renders the night hours lonely.
On this day,
　　We pray for all those whose loved ones
　　have lost their lives and too often their youth
　　to the dreaded disease of AIDS.
　　We pray for those we have named and for the unnamed,
　　the known and the unknown,
　　who have no quilts of remembrance.
　　We pray for all those in this world who suffer.
　　We bring before you for healing the people of Africa.
　　in grateful thanks for ears that hear our prayer.
Holy God,
　　In the face of human failure and tragedy, we hardly know how to pray.
We pray for the souls of the dead and we weep with the sorrowing families
who will never again be whole. We pray as well for those whose choice of
violence we neither understand nor accept. We acknowledge anew that
violence is always a faithless response.

　　Most of all, we pray for ourselves, that we might renew our passion
for love, for life, and for compassion. Guide us to make compassion a clear,
luminous, and dynamic force in our polarized world.

　　We pray as well for Chautauqua that we might continue our witness
to the wisdom that manifests itself in the rhythm of life that we experience here—the lush of summer green, the ripple of our beloved lake that
moves seamlessly into the autumn colors, a time when nature rests, only

to bloom again and again. And yes, winter comes and we are weary with the cold and give thanks for the warmth of our fires. Without fail the tulips burst their bulbs and nature teaches us year after year that God is good. Seasons come and go and life is precious and life is rich. In the face of these gifts we dare never choose violence or hatred, but ever and always seek peace.

✛

Dear God,
Be with us now as we bring before you those who stand in need of prayer.
    We pray today especially for people who have
    experienced unimaginable tragedy,
    for those who grieve in the face of lives too early taken.
    We pray for all whose lives will be forever changed
    by the horror of senseless, unexpected terror.
    Our hearts are stirred by undeserved suffering and we are awakened
        to those whose names we do not know
        and whose faces we will never see,
        who suffer in places unfamiliar to us.
We give thanks, O God, for feelings that can be stirred,
    For compassion that comes alive in us.
    So we pray for the courage to respond to the gift of compassion;
        may it mold us and move us to care more deeply
        to love more expansively,
        to share more generously the blessings that are ours.
    As we shudder at the shock of lives cut short,
        we are surprised by our unexpected reaction to a tragedy
        that does not touch our lives directly;
        we face anew the ties that bind us.
    We are one people bound together, interdependent, all children of God.
        Today we pray for a deepened commitment to a world
            where all are fed and housed and clothed and freed.
    We pray for the safety of children in all times and all places.
Holy one, open us to the power of compassion,
    Remind us that peace is not the grand gesture
    but the simply invisible, improbable embrace of those we find
    difficult to love.
Amen.

✠

Holy God,
    Giver of Life,
    You love us as a father and
        care for us as a mother.
    You dared to come to us to share
        our life as a brother.
    For all this—and so much more—
        we are grateful.
    We confess before you
        and one another
    that we fail to live as your children
        bound together in love.
    We fear that if we do your will
    we will lose our carefully charted way.
    Is the life you gave us ours to own
        or are we to trust you, God, to guide us in your way?
    So with uncertainty we sing

> *Take my life, and let it be*
> *consecrated, Lord, to thee.*
> *Take my moments and my days;*
> *let them flow in ceaseless praise.*[16]

Creator God,
    You have given us many talents
        and we have trained them
        and tended them well.
    We give thanks for voices that
        touch the deepest,
        most sacred places in our souls.
    Yet we confess that we give ourselves
        too much credit and measure out
        too carefully when and where
        to share our talents.
    Help us to trust you, God,
        to risk putting our gifts
        in your hands.

---

16. "Take My Life" by Frances Ridley Havergal, 1874, altered; music by Henri A. César Malan, 1827; tune: Hendon.

With uncertainty we sing

> *Take my feet, and let them be*
> *swift and beautiful for thee;*
> *Take my voice, and let me sing*
> *always, only, for my King,*
> *always, only for my King.*

God of Mystery and Majesty,
    Giver of all life,
    you have created for your children
        a universe of beauty and plenty,
        intricately designed—
    spectacular in its abundance.
We are in awe of the majesty that
        surrounds us, yet we confess that
        we fail to offer our own resources
        with the same generosity of spirit
        that is inherent in your creation.
So with uncertainty we sing

> *Take my lips, and let them be*
> *filled with messages from thee;*
> *Take my silver and my gold,*
> *not a mite would I withhold,*
> *not a mite would I withhold.*

Holy God,
    Your spirit enters our uncertain selves
        and we risk our perceived security,
        ready to entertain the possibility that
        we might be safe enough in your love
        that we could dare to be extravagant
        with the life you have given us.
So we timidly offer to you ourselves
    and await blessings not of our creation.
Take my love.

✠

God of mystery and majesty
> Holy God, Holy and Mighty One, Holy Immortal One,
> Creator of all,
> You are our God and we are your people.
> Holy God, your greatness is beyond our comprehension.
> We come before you in awe,
> confessing that too often we believe that we know
> what only you can know.
> We make decisions based on our limited understanding.
> We fail to seek your guidance and your people suffer.

Christe, eleison; Christe, eleison; Christe, eleison

Holy God, Creator of all,
> Holy and Mighty One,
> We are stunned at the intricacy and interdependence of your
> creation and confess our failure to care for every creature, even as
> you have cared for us.
> You call us to gentleness and affection, to love, to joy and peace.
> Our ambitions take hold and we lose our way.
> Return us to your path . . .

Christe, eleison; Christe, eleison; Christe, eleison

Holy God, Holy Immortal One,
> You claim us—each one of us—as your people.
> We know our selves all too well and in that knowing
> we are mystified by your enduring love.
> You love us even when we do not love ourselves.
> You call us out of the darkness of our despair
> and we come to know you, God,
> and in knowing, we dare to open our selves to one another.
> In your embrace we are made whole again and again.
> Forgive our failure to accept the mystery of your enabling love . . .

Kyrie, eleison; Kyrie, eleison; Kyrie, eleison

✜

God of yesterday, today, and tomorrow,
    We come grateful for the year just past.
    We come acknowledging that our gratefulness
    is at times shallow and short lived.
    We recognize our limited capacity for loving-kindness.
    Deep in our souls we come seeking the more excellent way
    that is your way, the way of love.
    We bow on bended knee in full recognition of your grace.
    We are grateful for your tolerance of our failure to live as agents
    of your vision for a just and peaceful world.
    We come to the safety and beauty and wonder of this place.
    Too often we fail to want this wonder
    for all your children everywhere.
    We are too often startled by your bold vision
    for a common humanity,
    a people made one, and find it too fanciful, too idealistic,
    too impractical for our goal-oriented lives.
    We confess that our embrace is too small, too passionless,
    too limited to those like us.
    In your generosity you call us to cradle the whole creation.
Dear God, we are your people and you are our God.
    We know that we are loved and forgiven
    and in that awakening lies the bright hope of tomorrow.

Loving God,
  You have told us in a thousand tongues, in thankless acts of mercy,
  in sacrifice to bold for us to comprehend that you are our God and
  we are your people.
  We confess that we too often feel empty, unloved, unable to receive
  the great truth you would have us see.
  So now and here:

> *Silently now I wait for thee,*
> *ready, my God, thy will to see.*
> *Open my eyes, illumine me, Spirit divine!*[17]

Merciful God,
  You have loved us unconditionally.
  You have prayed that a love so amazing,
  so divine, might free us to love one another.
  We confess that our fears and our animosities clog the arteries
  of our hearts, magnificently created to give life.
  Free us from the burdens of anxiety and the self-doubt stirred by fear.
  Let the even beat of love flow through our veins.
  So now and here:

> *Silently now I wait for thee,*
> *ready, my God, thy will to see.*
> *Open my eyes, illumine me, Spirit divine!*

Holy God,
  Your love is greater than we can comprehend—
  so great that too often we just refuse to believe
  that such a love is possible, a love that is not piety,
  a love that does not keep score,
  a love that forgives the most painful indiscretions.
  We crucify you and still you love us.
  You are our teacher and we your faithful students,
  afraid to take the risk of loving even

---

17. "Open My Eyes, That I May See," words and music by Clara Scott, 1895;
tune Open My Eyes.

when there is no evidence of return,
too fearful to try peace because battle is more easily measured,
too timid of heart,
too rigid of mind to give love a chance.
So now and here:

> *Silently now I wait for thee,*
> *ready, my God, thy will to see.*
> *Open my eyes, illumine me, Spirit divine!*

Holy God, Source of all love,
    You have so loved us that you sent your son Jesus,
    who, on the night of his betrayal,
    gave his disciples a new commandment,
        To love one another even as they were loved.
    Like the disciples of old, we confess our inability
    to grasp a love so amazing, so divine.
    We withhold ourselves from others.
    We fail to love as we were taught.
    In your mercy, grant us forgiveness.
Holy God, Source of all love,
You created us for community,
    to live together in a garden of love and delight.
    Forgive us for losing our way,
    for dividing ourselves into different flocks,
    for failing to recognize that where there is one shepherd,
    there is one flock.
    In your mercy, forgive us for losing our way.
Holy God, Source of all love,
    You teach through writings that have survived the ages,
    that love never ends, that love is patient and kind,
    not envious or boastful or arrogant.
    Forgive us for our too easy "I love you,"
    our too shallow self-giving.
    Forgive us for keeping score,
    for storing up the wrongs instead of searching
    for the hidden hurts that might be healed.
    In your mercy, grant us forgiveness.
Holy God, Source of all love,
    You commanded us to love our neighbor as ourselves.
    Forgive us for being too hard on ourselves,
    for refusing to see the gracious gifts we have been given,
    for failing to accept our humanity,
    for hiding our hurts from those who would be fed
    by helping and loving us,

for not loving ourselves enough to love our neighbor.
In your mercy, grant us forgiveness.
Holy God, Source of all love,
You offer us a love that does not let us go.
Those who teach in your name
remind us that nothing can separate us from your love.
Forgive us for thinking we can be God,
help us to acknowledge the limits of love,
and, within those limits, stretch us to risk all that we are
and all that we have on behalf of a world made whole,
a world where all are fed and freed, housed and clothed.
In your mercy, hold us in your everlasting arms and teach us to love.
Amen.

✠

O God of us all,
>> You love us as a father,
>> care for us as a mother,
>> came to share our life as a brother.
> We confess before you and one another our failure to
>> live as your children, sisters and brothers bound together in love.
> Like the disciples of old, we grow weary with all that must be done
> with the seemingly endless needs that present themselves
> before our eyes.
> We live in a world grown near and small.
>> We see war as daily news and we hear of the hunger
>> of nameless and faceless children.
> Our hearts grow cold with the burden of it all.
> Surely we are entitled to a time of rest and the peace
> of an uninterrupted life.
> Like the disciples of old we hear ourselves saying,
>> Let them take care of themselves, at least for a brief moment.
> But you call to us, your disciples in this time and place.
> You remind that we have chosen to go by the name of Christian.
>> It is a choice that frames our ethical response.
> You breathe life into our hearts and you remind us,
>> as you did the disciples of old, that we are to feed your children.
Thank you, God, for interrupting our well planned lives,
> yes, even our peaceful vacations.
We confess our weariness,
> our very need for renewal.
We need to be loved by one another;
> forgive us when we forget that our love extends to all those that you
> call your children.
We too need to be fed;
> we who never know hunger crave spiritual food.
We are grateful for your church when in faithfulness the word is preached,
> the scriptures are shared,
> and music is sung and played with a passion that feeds our souls
> and despite our weakness never turns us away.

Our needs are met by a God who never says to us,
Take care of yourselves; I am too busy.
Thank you for reminding us that you have instilled in us the capacity for
compassion.
Set us free from a past that we cannot change.
Open us to a future in which we can be changed.
God of timeless love, grant us grace.

✠

❋ 9 ❋

NOW THANK WE ALL OUR GOD

Help us to rekindle the flame of hope deep within us. O God, you call us to a life of celebration in the midst of deepest sorrow, hidden yearnings, and irreverent joy. You call us to dance and we fear we will look foolish. You call us to sing and we protest we have no voice. You call us to love and we ask who, how, when, how much, how deep, how intimate. Your arms enfold us and we are safe to come alive. God of unlimited love, we pray, teach us, show us your way. Open us to joy.

✥

A THANKSGIVING

Gracious God,
For the gifts of life and lake,
 for entrusting into our hands your most precious creation,
 we are more than grateful.
We are humbled by your trust,
 by your expectation that we will tend these gifts faithfully.
 With trepidation we acknowledge your expectation
 that we will protect your treasured gifts from harm.
With humility we respond with our promise
 to preserve your gifts for all people;
 for generations yet to be born,
 for children whose names we will never know,
 whose faces we will never see.
We pray this day that we might
 be claimed anew by your love and
 transformed by your generosity.
Grant us courage and instill in us a passion for tenderness
 as we awaken anew to the demands of Thanks-Giving.

✛

Gracious God,
    It's spring—thank you! The flowers bloom.
    Renewal is in the air, the sun shines on our darkness.
    Hope springs eternal.
    We are grateful.
Loving God,
    We pray for all who have finished life's course.
    You gather up the saints into your eternal embrace.
    We honor these lives that bless us in their living
    and inspire us in our remembering.
Loving God,
    We pray for all who are ill, struggling, sad, searching.
    You offer healing to those who suffer,
    spiritual strength to those too self-absorbed,
    wisdom to the young,
    and energy to the treasured elderly.
Loving God,
    We pray for our world:
    For those whose names we do not know,
    whose faces we will never see.
    Instill in us a yearning for peace—
    a yearning so strong that we let love replace fear
    and dare to take the risk to trust
    that love is the most powerful force in the world.
Creator God,
    Your will for your children—all your children,
    is that they will love and be loved.
    And so we rejoice in the gift of all the newborn babies,
    in love that blossoms and crowds out
    all sensible reason to hesitate and worry and wonder,
    in ties that bind for day or month or year;
    for parents and children who give strength to one another,
    who teach through trials
    and reward in unexpected ways and places.

For all this and so much more, we are grateful.
And so we offer to your glory this place—
>   its beauty, its program, its preachers, its lecturers,
>   its artists and its music heard in chorus and orchestra,
>   in singers and strings and arias,
>   and in the rustle of leaves on age-old trees.

✤

CLOSING PRAYER

God of all our seasons,
God of all our years,
Make of each year a blessing.
Where there is sorrow, give us solace.
Where there is pain, give us strength.
Where there is joy, fill us with thanksgiving.
Where there is bitterness, transform us with your love.
God, who calls us to choose and cherish life,
    we are yours.
    We dare to risk a live of love and laughter.

PRAYER FOR THE CHAUTAUQUA FOUNDATION
75TH ANNIVERSARY—JUNE, 2012

Gracious God—you are generous beyond
    our capacity to comprehend.
Yet—in our own limited way—
    we grasp the meaning of generosity,
    of boundless love,
    and the power of your eternal embrace.
You call us out of ourselves
    into a world of need and possibility.
So to us, the gifted and the strong,
    God's call comes down through the ages.
    We hear the words of teachers, preachers, prophets, and disciples,
    who remind us that unto whom much is given,
    much is required.
On this night we celebrate all who have heard the call,
    all who have responded faithfully and courageously,
    with unbounded generosity.
We pray this night for Chautauqua, for our common future.
    May we become a beacon of hope in a war-weary world.
    Amen.

Creator God,

    Once again we come into your presence awed by the evident reality
that you know us well and love us still.

    We dare to ask once again, help us to love ourselves and one another.

God of mercy, we come to you amidst the din of a political season

    and amidst a flood of facts, we search for Truth.

    In the face of rumors of war we pray for peace, and as so often

    in tumultuous times, we are blessed by the words

    of the familiar hymn:

    Grant us wisdom,

    grant us courage

    for the living of these days.[18]

Even in the midst of all that is uncertain, we give thanks for

    human creativity—

    for dancers and musicians, for singers and actors and actresses,

    for painters and writers and preachers.

Finally, we give thanks for children who, when loved and cradled,

    and held as precious, are endearingly open

    to a life filled with possibilities.

    In their innocence they teach us and give us courage.

So we gather up our weary selves, and move with hope and passion

    to be a loving presence in an unjust world. Amen.

God of the ages,

    You are to most of us a mystery;

        to many an impossibility;

        to others, hope in the midst of dark and desperate situations.

    We pray to you knowing you love us not as a worker of miracles

    nor our personal go-to person in tough times.

    Rather we pray to you as ultimate planner who dared to risk it all

    by granting to each of us free will—you created us for partnership

    and placed in our hands and hearts the creation you love.

    So we come to you humbly seeking a blessing

---

18. "God of Grace and God of Glory," words by Harry Emerson Fosdick, 1930.

for our modest efforts to protect, preserve, and hold precious
the place you gave to us—Chautauqua.
We come to give thanks for the gifts given to us of imagination,
intelligence, generosity, compassion, and hope for a future beyond
our time (and place).
We acknowledge we are your people—you are our God
and we are grateful.
Believing in ourselves and our common efforts—
even knowing our limits—we place our work and our worry
in your hands and, unafraid, dare to pray, gracious God.
Thy will be done.
Amen.

Lord of bright mansions above and earthly challenges below, you are God of the whole of our lives. You know our most sparkling visions and our deepest despair. You know us well and love us still. You hear our prayers while they are yet forming in our hearts. We sigh and you respond. We whisper and you hear. We weep and you wipe away our tears. We come before you with unspoken prayers, thoughts too frightening to put into words.

Lord, hear our prayer.

Precious Jesus, at your birth your people sang, "Joy to the World." You were love come to earth and centuries later we still repeat the sounding joy. And when the shining star of Bethlehem struck fear into the hearts of the shepherds, you spoke the words we need today. Fear not. Fear not in an uncertain world, for in the face of an unpredictable future you said, I bring you good tidings of great joy. Today we pray once again and acknowledge that light always dispels the darkness and love always and forever overcomes fear and your word and your way open to us the path of life and joy.

Lord, hear our prayer.

We are your grateful people; we know that no need is too small, too insignificant, or too enormous. We pray for all those who close the door at night and sit alone in the shadows, lives previously more vital. We pray for renewal of spirit, especially for those mired in their own mistakes, in grief for risks not taken and love not given. Enfold them in your loving arms.

Help us to rekindle the flame of hope deep within us. O God, you call us to a life of celebration in the midst of deepest sorrow. You know our hidden yearnings and our reverent joys. You call us to dance and we fear we will look foolish. You call us to sing and we protest we have no voice. You call us to love and we ask who, how, when, how much, how deep, how big the risk, how intimate? Your arms enfold us and we are safe to come alive. God of unlimited love, we pray, teach us, show us your way. Open us to joy.

Remind us that the bright light of hope invites us to lay our burdens down and ready ourselves for the blessing you have in store.

Lord, hear our prayer.

We know that you are a tender God who cares for each of us in deeply personal ways. Jesus, you assure us that you are waiting and watching, that you know already the sadness of those who grieve. So today we pray as we name those who have died. We give thanks for their lives and pray for solace for those who still sob in silent moments. We pray for all those whose bodies are in need of healing.

Finally, gracious God, give us the courage to entrust to you all those things that are out of our hands, even our own living and dying.

Lord, hear our prayer.

Prayer for the Gifted and Strong

Creator God,
You have blessed us with your love.
>You have brushed us with stardust.
>You have called us to live for others.
>You have given us the challenge of plenty,
>>resources beyond our need.
Instruct us how to be a blessing,
>how to usher in a world of peace,
>how to craft from the stardust
>>a bright future for all your children.
Thank you, God, for your blessing.
>Teach us to bless one another.

✛

Gracious God,
> We confess what seems to be always with us:
> Broken things within us that seem never to mend,
> empty places within us that seem always to ache,
> things like buds within us that seem never to flower.

O God of love and grace,
> help us accept ourselves;
> for it is in loving ourselves that we are ennobled to love our neighbor.
> It is in accepting our shortcomings that we are ennobled
> to forgive others.
> It is in accepting our imperfections that we are saved
> from needing to be perfect.

In humility we pray,
> lead us to do those good and true things
> that bear witness to a generosity of spirit
> that your love for us has made possible.
> As much as can be, spirit God, fall afresh on us,
> mend us, fill us, and make us bloom.

We confess our need for your forgiveness God and pray today,
> enable us to turn from the way of violence and death;
> show us how to choose and cherish life.
> Amen.

Compassionate God,
> We kneel before you with awe.
> We behold your majesty with thankful hearts.
> We are overwhelmed by your embrace,
>> tender-hearted and eternal.
> Yet, you are not magic.
> You offer no quick fix for our hurts,
>> no potion to clear up our confusion,
>> no compass to set our life in the right direction.
> You do not spare us from sickness or pain or even death.
>> You do not make our choices for us.
> You knit us together in our mother's womb.

Compassionate God,
> You have searched us and know our innermost thoughts.
> With all our sins and our sorrows,
>> our secrets and our sadness,
>> our potential and our failures,
> you love us still.

You offer us the Balm in Gilead.
> You come to us in the deepest despairs,
>> in the darkest nights
>>> and still the troubled waters of our soul.
> Enfold us in the arms of your grace. Amen.

❋ IO ❋

HOPE AND HEALING

Let us pray in the name of
    God the merciful,
    God the compassionate.
We come before you today, your grateful people;
    in a world of uncertainty you offer to us the
    security of your presence.
In a world of illness and disease
    you bless us with your healing power.

In a time of war and violence you hold before us love—
    call us to a vision of peace.
In the presence of poverty and hunger
    you offer us a vision of generosity.
So on this day of hope and resurrection
    and in the name of the women who dared to
    believe the unbelievable,
in a time of hopelessness
    you offer eternal life.
    You feed our emptiness with the bread of life
    and we give thanks.
    Amen.

Creator God,

    Whose love for us is boundless,

    whose ways are beyond our understanding,

    whose creativity is greater than we can ever imagine,

    we bow before you at this common altar.

    We come in gratefulness and humility, yet with high expectation.

    We lay before you the concern of our hearts.

    We speak haltingly, for the anguish of our souls is too deep for words.

We open ourselves to you in full recognition that you already know

    our hidden sorrows,

    our most extravagant joys,

    our most fervent prayers.

We pray for those in this community

    who live with us now in our memories:

    Those we name in our hearts.

    We pray for all whose mornings begin with pain

    borne of illness or anxiety.

    Touch each and every one with your healing power.

We pray for all your people in this wide world,

    for those children who are born into loveless families,

    for all who go to bed hungry, who suffer from famine or flood,

    for all who face the violence born of terror, war, and bigotry.

        Bring justice. Grant peace. Amen.

⊹

Merciful God,
> You who created us for love,
> we give thanks this day
> for quiet acts of splendid courage,
> for mothers and fathers, sisters and brothers,
> husbands, wives, partners, neighbors, friends
> who have through acts of heroic loving
> saved lives, quieted pain, provided healing laughter.
> Their compassion breeds hope in a world
>> grown too easily cynical.

O God, hear us; hear our prayer.

Today we remember all those whom the world
> has crowned as heroes and heroines:
Preachers, presidents, artists, musicians.
They bear the burden of huge expectations,
> yet they wrestle with the knowledge
> of their own imperfection.
Help them not to take their press too seriously.
> Grant them the capacity to laugh.
Give them the gift of love from those who truly know them,
> and give to each one of us the maturity to know
>> that we are flawed,
>>> yet capable of glory.

O God, hear us; hear our prayer.

Eternal and Almighty God,
> Creator of ordinary people equipped for extraordinary tasks,
> we give you thanks for all your faithful people
> who have followed your will in a grand procession of praise
> throughout the world and down through the centuries.
> We hear their stories in the pages of scripture,
>> in the records of history,
>> in the recollections of our families,
>>> and in our own childhood memories.

As we remember these people,
    inspire us to rise to their ranks,
    to be bold as they were, and brave as well.

O God, hear us; hear our prayer.

God of unlimited love, we pray, teach us, show us your way.

Melt us, mold us, fill us, use us.

We pray today for all those who have more years in front of them
than behind them.
For the younger generation and those who come after them.
We do not so much pray that their way will be easy,
rather that it will be worth the struggle.
We pray for their strength and courage, for their love and laughter.
We pray that those of us who go before them
might have the wisdom to will to their generation
a world where peace is sought, barriers broken, bridges built.
Together may God grant us hearts of compassion
that we might reach out in sacrificial ways
To those unlike us, to those whose ways are not our ways.

Melt us, mold us, fill us, use us.

Finally, we pray for ourselves that we might trust you enough,
Creator God, to pray your will be done;
open us to the future you have envisioned for your children.

Melt us, mold us, fill us, use us.

✦

Merciful God,
    You are a God of miracles.
    You sent your son Jesus to give sight to the blind,
    to help the lame to walk,
        the deaf to hear, the dead to rise.
    Your love gives life, not death, the last word.
    You are a healing God.
    Your healing powers are readily available to all who pray,
        "Your will, not mine, be done."
    In the quiet of this moment, we pray for your healing wisdom.
        We pray for healing between all the warring nations.
        We pray for healing within our nation.
        We pray that the spirit of peace
        might move mightily across this hurting world.
        We pray for the poor that they might be fed.
        We pray for the rich that they might be moved to share.
        We pray for the races that they might see in each other
        the face of God.
        We pray for the church that all division might be healed,
          so that the world might believe.
    We pray that we might break age-old barriers and come at last to bow
        at one common altar where we might receive together
        the gifts of God
        for the people of God.
We pray especially for all who are in physical and psychic pain,
    all who face unknown illness,
    all who await the doctor's healing touch.
    We pray for doctors, nurses, hospitals, midwives, healers.
    We pray for all who grieve any loss of love or life.
    Amen.

Gracious God,
    You come to us in the midst of our disunity and our separation.
    Come, be with us now.
    For these few moments transform the Babel created from the
    conflicting claims of our lives.
    Make of the noise a sweet song of unity.
    Reach deep into our souls and mend all that is broken.
    Heal the wounds made raw by anger.
    Stir the passions grown cold from painful rejection.
    Still the fears that limit our enormous capacity for love.
    Calm our most inward selves that we might sing:

> *It is well (it is well) with my soul (with my soul),*
> *it is well, it is well with my soul.*

Lord of bright mansions above and earthly challenges below:
    You are God of the whole of our lives—
    The most sparkling visions and the deepest despair.
    You know us well and love us still.
    You hear our prayers while they are yet forming in our hearts.
    We sigh and you respond.
    We whisper and you hear.
    We weep and you wipe away our tears.
    We come before you with deep unspoken prayers and
    we are made whole in the knowledge that sins can be forgiven and
    all things made new.
    Calm our most inward selves that we might sing:

> *It is well (it is well) with my soul (with my soul),*
> *it is well, it is well with my soul.*

We pray for our lives together.
    Meld and mold this beautiful place that sings and paints
    and acts and plays in your creation.
    Open our eyes that we might envision your future,
    not ours for ourselves,
    for our families,
    for every place we call home.

Now, loving God,

Into your hands we commit all the problems which seem insoluble, in
the sure and certain hope, for in you is our trust.

Here and now we lay all in your hands.

All love, all glory be unto you for ever and ever as we sing:

> *It is well (it is well) with my soul (with my soul),*
> *it is well, it is well with my soul.*[19]

✛

---

19. "It Is Well with My Soul," words by Horatio Gates Spafford, 1873; tune, Ville
Du Havre.

God of the ages and architect of a future yet to be revealed,
>   You have been our help in ages past and hope for years to come.
>   We confess that our anxieties grow,
>   our fears unsettle us,
>   we fail to acknowledge that only in your love
>   are we sheltered from the stormy blast.

From everlasting you are God, to endless years the same.
>   We hear these words and wrestle with the enormity of their meaning.
>   Why is it, O God, that we so firmly believe that our defenses
>   against an uncertain world are in our hands alone?
>   Forgive us for our failure to receive your love,
>   to rest easy in the knowledge that sufficient is your arm alone and
>   only in the shadow of your throne will we dwell secure.
>   Grant to us the peace that can come when we acknowledge that only
>   your defense is sure.

Gracious God ,we affirm with hope your presence in the world.
>   We confess that when trouble comes
>   we fret and fuss and blame and deny.
>   We close doors and turn away good help
>   when all we would have to do is ask.
>   We forget that time will bear us all away.

Forgive us and be our guide while troubles last, and our eternal home.

✠

Prayer for the Dying

Great and Good God,
Your Son, Jesus, said,
"Come unto me all who labor and are heavily burdened
    and I will give you rest."
Today I am weary and in pain.
I have loved the life you so generously gave to me.
I have tried, to the best of my ability, to be faithful.
Now, O Lord, I am ready to lay my burdens down.
Receive me into your loving arms.
I feel the presence of your angels around me.
I reach out my hands to you and pray that the saints
    will welcome me in peace.
I pray today for safe passage into an unknown tomorrow
    and I put my trust in Jesus.
Watch over my children and grandchildren.
Love them as I do.
Grant them a bright future. Amen.[20]

✛

---

20. Prayer printed in modified form in Joan Brown Campbell, *Living into Hope* (Woodstock, VT: SkyLight Paths Publishing, 2010), 112.

II

THE COMMON CUP

The common cup is a call to unity.

Creator God,
We come before you this day as your grateful community.
We gather at this common altar,
  and in the midst of your creation we come—one flock, one shepherd.
We give thanks for our unity with one another
  and with the whole of the created order.
It is this unity that joins us to one another,
  to all that has gone before and all that is yet to be.

We dare to bring to you our hopes, our dreams,
    our fears, our disappointments, and our joy.
Help us to trust a way that may not be our way,
    a future that is beyond our mortal capacity to envision.

Oh, God, hear us, hear our prayer.

We confess to you this day that too often we pray with a plan in mind
for your response.
We pray more times than we can count,
"Your will be done,"
    but truth be told, we must confess
    we have our own plans, our own agenda.

Oh, God, hear us, hear our prayer.

We pray today for your world.
    Wherever there are civil wars,
    remind your people, God, that they are one.
    We pray today for an end to enmity
    between husbands and wives, parents and children,
    between those who call themselves religious.
    Heal all our warring ways.
    Stir our souls that we might bring peace to all lands,
    between all people.

Oh, God, hear us, hear our prayer.

We pray at last for ourselves, for all who are ill:
    Where discouragement has made its claim,
    give us a new usefulness.
    Where pride distorts, touch us with corrected sight.
    Where guilt overwhelms,
    lead us to repentance and guard us from despair.
    Stand watch with the undecided, the confused, those who hurt,
    and give us good reasons to smile, even on the worst days.
    Let your love so prevail among us
    that we may truly count all others precious,

and grant us such courage that we may always bear witness
to the truth that sets all people free.

> **Oh, God, hear us, hear our prayer.**

God, our Creator,
> by whose mercy and might the world turns safely
> into darkness and returns again to light,
> we give into your hands our unfinished tasks,
> our unsolved problems and our unfulfilled hopes,
> knowing that only those things which you bless will prosper.
> To your great love and protection we commit each other
> and for all whom we have prayed,

> **Oh, God, hear us, hear our prayer.**

✠

Merciful God,
 We know that you love us and that you call us to fullness of life.
 You command us to care for one another and for your creation.
 Forgive us
  when we hesitate to love with abandon,
  to risk breaking the rules to save the suffering ones.
 Forgive us when we hesitate to give of ourselves,
  fearful we will lose our way and forget that you are the way,
  the truth, the light.
 Forgive us when we fail to walk lightly on the earth,
  forgetting that this is your gift to us and to generations to come.
Holy God,
 You have bound us together in a common life.
Today we pray
 in spite of our tendency to pull apart,
 our tenacity to hold on to our old ways.
 Call us back together again and again.
 Welcome us home and embrace us with your promise of
 forgiveness.
 Help us to remember that your embrace is forever within our reach.
 You never tire nor lose patience in your willingness to show us
 again and again the power of love,
 the healing energy of forgiveness.

Holy One, you are our Shepherd and we are your flock.

Restorer of our souls, you direct us into right paths
and yet we confess that we stray from the way set before us.
Forgive us our fierce determination to go our own way.

Holy One, you are our Shepherd and we are your flock.

You assure us that we need not want.
You protect us from our enemies.
You seed the earth with fruits and vegetables to overflow our tables.
Goodness and mercy are your gifts for today, tomorrow, forever.
Forgive us our lack of trust,
Our hoarding your generosity only for ourselves.
Teach us to share your bounty.
You are our Shepherd; we need not want.
Free us from our wanting.

Holy One, you are our Shepherd and we are your flock.

You embrace your vast creation.
You know your sheep.
You call each one by name
and all made in your image are yours—one shepherd, one flock.
Forgive us for dividing the flock,
for naming some more precious than others,
for believing that we have special claim
to the Shepherd's comfort and care.
And when we believe we are threatened,
remind us that even though we walk
through the valley of the shadow of death,
we need not fear.
Forgive us our excuses for war,
our penchant for retaliation.
Remind us that all God's children dwell
    in the house of the Lord forever.

✠

God of majesty and glory,
>   You have set before your people
>   visions of wonder and salvation,
>   deserts that blossom,
>   weak hands that grow strong,
>   a wilderness where waters break forth,
>   everlasting joy,
>   a way no longer watered by tears.
>   Even with the joy of it all,
>   we confess that we hesitate to place our lives in your hands.
>   Stir our complacent souls until we sing with confidence,

We are God's people.

God of mercy,
>   Your ways are healing ways.
>   You set before your people a vision of wholeness,
>   blind eyes that are opened,
>   deaf ears unstopped,
>   the lame that leap like deer.
>   We confess that we yearn for the wholeness of life,
But too often we are unwilling to live with the consequences
of eyes that are
opened to injustice,
>   ears that can hear the cries of the hungry,
>   limbs that might carry us beyond the shelter
>   or security of our own kind.
>   O God, strengthen us for the journey of faith.

We are God's people.

God, you hold the whole world in your hands.
>   We sing of your greatness,
>   we read of your power,
>   we pray and ask for your attention in matters small and great,
>   yet we confess we all too often try to make you in our image.
>   Your love is too large for us to imagine.

We confess that we make you small enough for us to grasp.
>   We define your flock as our own kind,
>   we separate, alienate, set aside.
>   You integrate and unite and make whole.
>   Open us to the fullness of your grace.
>   Great Shepherd, you have called us for unity.

>   **We are God's people.**

(Based on Isaiah 35)

✛

Communion Prayer

Holy God, Holy Immortal One,
Giver of all life, spirit of hope,
>   you sustain us in our struggles;
>   you challenge us when we are self absorbed.
You forgive us when we lose our way;
>   you love us when we do not love ourselves.
You call us out of the darkness of our despair.
You remind us that we are yours—
>   created for hope and joy,
>   wired for compassion and tenderness and peace.
So we lift this cup and drink this wine with a toast of grateful thanks
>   and we promise again to receive you as spirit,
>   to accept your life-affirming gifts.

SHARING A SIGN OF GOD'S PEACE

We have seen our world torn apart by wars
and rumors of war.
Conflict abounds.
Religion too often divides,
families break apart,
and love too timid fails to heal.
We are called by our creator
to live in peace with one another.
So in this moment
let us set aside all animosities that plague us
and prejudices that divide us
and for the sake of our children and grandchildren
let us offer now to one another the sign of peace.
We do this not as a simple gesture of friendship,
but as a sign that we wish to be at peace with all people.
We look into the face of a stranger,
and there we see the face of God.
Let us join in this act of reconciliation
and prayerfully greet one another
with the ancient words said round the world:
"The peace of God be with you." Please respond: "And also with you."

✠

COMMUNION PRAYER

God of all creation, lover of humanity,
> We, your faithful children gather once again
>> to receive in a simple piece of bread your promise of life eternal.
> We remember and celebrate the short-lived victory of Palm Sunday
>> and prepare ourselves for the sadness and pain of Good Friday.
> You guide us in our own lives to live
>> through the victories and the disappointments of life.
> You promise us all that nothing can separate us from your love
>> and it is that promise that points to the resurrection.
So we live with courage and hope
>> and give thanks time and again
>> for the bread of life that turns hurt into hope.
>> Amen.

Eternal God,

 Whose image lies in the hearts of all people,

 we live among people whose ways are different from ours,

 whose faiths are foreign to us,

 whose tongues are unintelligible to us.

 Our instinct too often is to separate ourselves

 from those we do not understand.

 We build walls of division and create misunderstanding.

We pray for the courage to tear down those walls

 and for the imagination to see in all people a partner for peace.

 Help us to remember that you love all people with your great love,

 that all religion is an attempt to respond to you,

 that the yearnings of other hearts are much like our own

 and are known to you.

Stir in church leaders and laity alike a passion for unity.

 Remind us that you prayed your vision

 that we might be the one people we were created to be.

 Help us to recognize you in unlikely places and faces,

 in acts of loving kindness,

 in words of truth,

 in the beauty that surrounds us.

Make us newly aware that love is the greatest force

 the world has ever known.

 Hatred has had its way with us too long

 in a world created for the well-being of all your children,

 a world rich in resources enough to nurture every child,

 every nursing mother, every worker, banker, lawyer,

 doctor, teacher, artist, politician, and preacher.

Teach us the way of justice.

 Show us the path of peace.

Today, we bring to this common altar our heartfelt prayer for peace

 in a world where fifty-eight wars rage,

 where deeply held beliefs are twisted and turned

 until love and justice are lost in self-serving acts of terror.

We pray this day for your healing power
    to come upon all the brokenness in our personal lives and our
    nation's life,
    in the life of our religious institutions,
    and most of all in our world.
    Let us be prayerful as we wait for the spirit to move us
    to renewed places of compassion.
Let us lift our unspoken, soul-deep common prayer
for the peace of the world.

✠

Merciful God,
    You are a God of miracles.
    You sent your son Jesus to give sight to the blind,
        to help the lame to walk,
        the deaf to hear,
        the dead to rise.
    Your love gives life, not death, the last word.
    You are a healing God.
    Your healing powers are readily available to all
        who have the courage to pray,
        "Your will, not mine, be done."
    In the quiet of this moment,
    we pray for your healing wisdom.
    We pray for healing between all the warring nations.
    We pray for healing within our nation.
    We pray that the spirit of peace might move mightily
        across this hurting world.
    We pray for the poor that they might be fed.
    We pray for the rich that they might be moved to share.
    We pray for the races that they might look in each other's eyes
    and see the face of God.
    We pray for the church that all division might be healed,
    so that the world might believe.
    We pray that we might break down age-old barriers
        and come at last to one common altar
        where we might receive together the gifts of God
        for the people of God.
    We pray especially this week for all who are in physical
        and psychic pain,
        all who face unknown illness,
        all who await the doctor's healing touch.
    We pray for doctors, nurses, hospitals, midwives, healers all.
    We pray for all who grieve any loss of love or life
        that their hearts might be mended
        and new life and love enriched by treasured memories.

Our most heartfelt prayers are for those who grieve
    from misplaced words of hate or anger,
    for distances between parents and children,
    for love offered and not received.
We pray for all who give love to all others,
    for children whose happy faces make us smile,
    for husbands and wives,
    for lovers and partners and friends,
    for pastors, teachers, and healers.
Grant them courage that they might stand strong in the face of harm,
    that they by their witness might overcome
        all efforts to hurt or destroy.
We pray, merciful God, that love might have its way,
that we open ourselves to the possibility
    that your healing, not understood by us,
    might bring us the peace we seek.
Amen.

❊ 12 ❊

WALKING TOGETHER—PEOPLE OF FAITH

This picture of Sister Joan Chittister and Salena Abedin at the meeting of the Global Peace Initiative of Women stirs my soul. Here are two brilliant, committed women, one Muslim, one Christian, both strong voices for peace and for justice, women whose gifts and graces can and have broken down barriers and are sign and symbol that walking together is both powerful and faithful.

JEWISH PARABLE FROM RABBI CHAYIM OF TSANZ

A man wandering in the forest for several days finally encountered another. The man called out, "Brother/Sister, show me the way out of this forest."

The women replied, "Brother, I too am lost. I can only tell you this. The ways I have tried lead nowhere. They have only led me astray. Take my hand and let us search for the way together."

The rabbi would add, so it is with us when we go our separate ways. We may go astray. Let us, people of every faith, join hands and look for the way together.

The wise words of an ancient rabbi remind us that we do not walk alone. In these days marked by destructive polarization, we are called to join hands and hearts as we search for the way together, a way where people of every faith are joined together as a sign of light in the darkness.

✣

Loving God,
    Your reach is broad, your vision bold,
    your love deeper than the deepest ocean,
    wider than the universe we know.

    Forgive us the limits of our loving.
    Forgive us the timidity of our vision.
    Forgive us our special pleading.
    Reserving you for us and our kind.

Eternal God,
    Your image lies in the hearts of all people.
    You have given life to us and to people
    whose ways are different from ours,
    whose faiths are foreign to us,
    whose languages are unintelligible to us.

Holy God, Holy Immortal One,
    You created us for community,
    for wholeness and for peace.
    You surrounded us with beauty and plenty.
    You gave us one another to love, cherish and comfort.
    You set the stars in the midnight sky,
    You brought light into deepest night.
    You prayed for an end to our senseless divisions, our familial fights.
    You instructed us always to choose life.

Forgive us our fragmentation,
    our failure to know that you are God,
    capable of embracing even those we do not know or understand.
Forgive us for claiming that we alone
    have favor in your eyes.
Forgive us, O God, the fears that reside in the deep
    recesses of our broken hearts.
Help us to recognize you in the words of truth,
    the things of beauty,
    the actions of love around us.

Almighty God,
 We are your grateful people,
 and we are reminded.
 In compassion God forgives us.
 Enable us to turn from the way of violence and death.
 Show us how to choose and cherish life.

✛

Almighty and ever-loving God,
    It is with profound and deeply felt thanksgiving
    that we come into your presence.
    Hear now the prayers of your people,
    in the midst of the beauty of this place,
    in the midst of plenty and peace,
    there is pain and sorrow, hurts that have not healed,
    and a world that cries out for peace.

Here in this place so far away from the din of the worldly conflict,
    we pray today, O God, for the peace of the world.
    We pray for Africa, torn apart by internal conflicts born
    out of years of colonial rule.
    We pray for Africa, where young women and men die of AIDS
    as the world comes late to seek a solution.
    We pray for those Jews, Christians, and Muslims in the Middle East
    whose history washes over them and makes of peace a prayer,
    a hope, a dream but not yet a reality.
God, open our eyes that we might hear the call to peace
    that is at the heart of every faith.
Help them and us to transcend our carefully crafted differences.
    Let us reach toward one another, people of all faiths and of no faith.
    Help us to see the rich variety of experience,
    the gifts we bring to one another.
We pray to you that people of all faiths may enjoy the freedom
to set forth their convictions with integrity
    and yet listen to one another with humility that faith might be
    a beacon for peace,
    might perform a reconciling ministry in a world divided
    by suspicion and misunderstanding.
    Bring healing to those places where religious intolerance
    fractures community.
Lord, you know the secrets of our hearts, the pain of our souls,
the joy of our loving.
    Hold us in your loving arms and grant us peace.
    Amen.

Loving God, Almighty and most gracious,
We come before you in the full knowledge that you know us,
    no doubt better than we know ourselves.
    We know we cannot hide from you.
    You know our sorrows and our sins,
    yet you claim us as your very own.
We come to this time of prayer with sighs too deep for words.
Despite our limitations we pray today for people of faith
and of no faith the world around.
We pray that in every land and in every heart,
faith might be marked by love and hope and generosity and acceptance
of the many ways we seek God.
We pray that we might open our hearts to the miracle that faith
is not defined by one religion more than another,
    when a Sikh temple is burned
       and a mosque is destroyed
         and a synagogue graffitified in ugly language.
    So we pray today for the community of faith,
    for all who see God in one another.
    for all whose hearts are open to those whose ways are different from
    their own.
Stir in us the radical possibility that your children might love one another
    enough for peace to break through hardened hearts,
    for hope to be born anew in those for whom life is unbearable sorrow,
    for the signs of faith to have open hearts, open minds, and a
    yearning to embrace that which we do not fully understand.
Holy God—Holy Immortal One,
    Mark us with a sign of a faith-filled life.
    Disturb our certainty.
    Mark us as a people of hope and love,
    that we might claim faith that flows through all the world
    like a river . . .
    that knows no boundaries.

✠

Creator God,
We bow before you this moment, people of many faiths.
> We give thanks for all that we hold in common,
>> a shared belief that love is the most powerful force
>>> the world will ever know,
a shared passion for life, full and free for all God's children everywhere,
> a universal tear for suffering borne of our warring madness,
>> and a fervent prayer for peace with justice.
We bow before you in grateful thanks for the plenty that
blesses our living day after day.
We are mindful that unto whom much is given, much is required.
In the name of the one we hold as holy,
> we offer our lives in the service of love and peace.
Amen.

✠

God of mystery,

Down through the ages we your children have sought to understand you. The enormity of your being is beyond our comprehension. Your capacity to love in the face of generations of challenges that would wilt the patience of most every parent astounds and humbles us.

We cannot see you completely in the ageless stories of your people. We glimpse you in the sacred texts that tell your story and set before us heroes and heroines who, like us, are but flawed human beings. Yet in these stories we come to know people you love, ordinary people you have called to extraordinary tasks, people who despite their inadequacies have responded to God's call.

And, miracles of miracles, your people cannot be contained in any one sacred book more than in another and, oh, my God, there is so much for us to learn if we will but open ourselves to the wideness of your mercy.

We walk among people who are like us and yet unlike us. We marvel at the variety of your creatures, at the diversity of stories yet to be written.

Loving God, we pray you will give us the passion and the courage to see beyond the familiar—delighting in our own house of faith, yet curious enough to explore the rooms where we have never been.

So we pray:

We pray for the community of people all over the world

who seek you in countless and mysterious ways,

who fervently desire to draw near to you,

who place their hope in your steadfast love and abounding mercy,

and who listen for your voice through rituals and symbols

that we do not know or understand.

We pray, O God, for our global community where there are neighbors whose hopes grow dim in the torrential rains and winds of war,

of hunger and suffering, and of turmoil and corruption.

Wash away the pain and the confusion with the healing waters

of compassion, mercy, and justice.

Show us how to truly be their neighbors,

and to allow them to become ours.

Open us to ways that we cannot plan
but which you will show us, as we make it our intention to bring the
human family ever closer together in your reconciling love.
Finally, God,
in this sacred space,
we pray for the community of our families and friends with whom we
share the most intimate moments of our life.
Amen.

✠

Holy God,

We are grateful that you created us for relationships. Pour into our DNA the capacity to give and receive love. You gave us the commandments and capacity for compassion. We are grateful for families, especially for those whose lives touch ours in generous and knowing ways. They give us strength—they test our capacity for loving and forgiving. They teach us the art of compassion. We are thankful for families who are not captive to their own small circle of life but who in their loving nurture neighbors across the wideness of the world.

Forgive us when we fail to build up life for each and every one in your all-inclusive family. Transform our imperfect love, which too often destroys those relationships that would give life. Help us to love without fear and to embrace with tender passion—even and especially those who do not understand.

We pray as we risk trust and love that through our encounters we might catch a glimpse of your greatness and generosity.

Now we pray for those in our community who are ill. Grant them health and well-being. Now for those who have died and those who grieve, we pray for peace. Receive them into the communion of saints.

We ask all these things in the name of the one who taught us who is our neighbor, who showed us the way toward acceptance of others, and who led us to those who are strangers that we might become brothers and sisters. Amen.

ISHMAEL   HAGAR   ABRAHAM   SARAH   ISAAC

We come now to the Prayers of the People. This is the time we set aside for our special prayers for the world, for the nation, and for our own community. Today before we begin our prayers I must share with you an incident that has distressed our usually peaceful, welcoming community. Hear this as a recommitment to the unity of this congregation.

Yesterday, Rich Moschel, year-round Chautauqua resident and volunteer fireman, was inaugurated president of the Hebrew Congregation. We congratulate Rich; however, we are deeply saddened by an incident that marred this important occasion. When the Moschels stepped out of their house they discovered at their doorstep a large ceramic pig, a symbol of deep disrespect for Jewish people. Such signs of prejudice and hidden hatred are more than just a casual prank and are totally unacceptable in our Chautauqua community of shared respect. We speak of this at this time of prayer as an act of solidarity with the Jewish people on these grounds and as expression of our deep sadness at such behavior. For the one who is responsible we pray for forgiveness and for the strength to love.

God of all people, we pray for hope that brings light into the darkness.
  We pray for Rich Moschel and pray that he is surrounded
  with love and girded with strength. We pray as well for the
  Hebrew congregation
  and for people everywhere who experience the pain of fear
  created by prejudice.
  We pray for this community and we commit ourselves anew
  to be reunited with the family of Abraham.
Holy God, we pray today that you who created us for loving and caring
  might move among us that we might be infused with your love
  and offer that very love to all people.
We live among the richness of your creation,
  people whose languages we do not know,
  people different from ourselves,
  people who call to God by many names.
  May we be touched by your majestic gift of life to all your children
  and by your love that exceeds our capacity to imagine.
  We pray for wisdom for the living of these days.

Eternal God,
> Whose image lies in the hearts of all people,
> we live among people whose ways are different from ours,
> whose faiths are foreign to us,
> whose tongues are unintelligible to us.

> Help us to remember that you love all people
>> with your great love.

> Instill in our hearts a yearning for justice,
>> and a passion for peace.

Shepherd of all the sheep,
> Your scriptures tell us that where there is one Shepherd,
>> there is one flock.

> Yet we divide ourselves into separate folds,
>> and pridefully enshrine our differences.

> Renew in us today a vision of unity.

> Open all houses of worship to your will and your way,
>> and walk with us as we seek together
>> to respond to your prayer that we might be one.

And now, loving God, we dare to pray
> for those we love and hold dear.

We pray today for all who wrestle with the disappointments of religion,
> yet yearn for a life of faith.

And now in this moment of silence, hear our heartfelt and private petitions.

✛

Eternal God, in whose image we are created,
  Open our minds and our hearts that we might fathom
  the miracle of your love,
  the wideness of your mercy.
  Forgive us when we draw our image of you to resemble
  only me and mine.
  Shatter the illusion that our God plays favorites.
  Comfort us with the recognition that to God no one is a stranger.
  We live among people whose ways are different from ours,
  whose faiths are foreign to us, whose tongues are unintelligible to us.
  Forgive us for retreating to our comfort zone and
  open us to the blessings of the unfamiliar.
Help us, gracious God, to remember that you love all people
  with your great love.
  Forgive us when we fail to acknowledge that all religion is an
  attempt to respond to you, that the yearnings of other hearts
  are much like our own and are known to you.
We confess that blinded by our own needs and anxieties
  we fail to recognize you in the words of truth,
  the things of beauty, the actions of love,
  that speak to us from unexpected people and places.
O God of all the nations, Holy to people of every faith,
  forgive us whenever our love of you gets confused with our
  passion for the religion most familiar to us;
  rather, let our hearts beat with a faith that includes all of earth's people,
  a song of peace for their land and for ours.
  We pray for forgiveness for our failure to love as we have been loved.
  In spite of our tendency to pull apart,
  in spite of our tenacity in our old ways,
Loving God, you continue to call us back together again,
  showing us the true nature of forgiveness.
  God does not keep score of our wrongs
  or measure how far we have wandered.
God embraces and welcomes us. We are forgiven people.

✛

Almighty and ever-loving God,

We come into your presence this day, as on every day with thanksgiving—hear our prayers.

We pray for the world created by your hands and tended by your children of every race and tongue.

We pray for the gift of awareness that we might acknowledge our interdependence.

Help us, O God, to make decisions that will be a blessing
not only in the lives of those we love but in the lives of those
whose faces we will never see,
whose names we will never call.
Give us the heart for peace making and the soul for justice.
Almighty God, ever present, we ask your blessing on all your children.
But especially we pray for all who offer to you
the love and worship of their hearts.
For women and men of all faiths, all who believe in you
and seek to serve you by the light that you have granted to them.
Let the faith of each be deep enough to respect the faith of everyone.
Forgive us our divisions and our unhelpful distinctions.
Grant to churches, synagogues, and mosques
the unity for which Jesus prayed.

⊹

13

IMPOSSIBLE DREAMS—VISION AND IMAGINATION

You are without beginning and without end,
Source and Sustainer of all that is or has been or will be.

God who teaches us a faith that makes ordinary life
an extraordinary miracle,
We worship you with open hearts, lusty voices,
inquiring minds, and prayerful attitude.

God of surprises,
> Since the days of Sarah who birthed a child
> when more than ninety years of age,
> you continue to amaze us with impossible dreams
> that become reality.
> Forgive us our fear of surprises,
> our need to protect ourselves from disappointment and
> our failure to risk dreams of the seemingly impossible.
> Forgive us the limits our fears place on human potential.

God of dreams that stir our souls,
> help us to accept the surprise you have in store
> for those willing to open their hearts to the unfamiliar.
> Grant us the courage to believe that there is nothing
> too wonderful for you.

God of hope and promise,
> We cry out that we are but your ordinary people.
> You respond that we are equipped for extraordinary tasks.

Thanks be to you who says to us
> fear not, in an uncertain world, fear not the unpredictable future.
> Remember that the God of history bid us good tidings of great joy
> for all people in every time and space and place.

✠

Creator God,

You breathe life into us and we burst forth onto the stage that will be our life. You do not promise us a life without sadness or struggles or disappointment but you give to us the capacity for joy—for hope. In age after age you call on us to dream impossible dreams.

Today we give thanks for the artists among us who touch our soul and remind us of a courage buried deep inside our rational, ordered lives.

We give thanks today for musicians whose instruments and voices can bring us to tears and cause us to dance and rejoice. They remind us that our emotions are your gift and can be trusted.

Our tired bodies watch dancers soar and in our imagination we are young again and all things are possible.

We stand back from magnificent works of art—sculpture, paintings, architecture—and marvel and we are touched in places that have grown dormant from an overabundance of reason. And, loving God, we catch anew a glimpse of your vision for your world—your children.

We walk into the theater, we settle into our seats and fasten our seat belts for actors and actresses to take us deep inside ourselves, and we are challenged anew to run where the brave dare not go.

And we are renewed as the gifts of artists touch us soul deep and your presence, Creator God, is felt again.

We risk anew the possibility that impossible dreams, like Peace, like Love, like Courage, like Hope, are within our reach.

✛

God of History, we hear you speaking.

> You stir our imagination.
>
> Your prophets and teachers have set down your words.
>
> Through the ages your peoples' closed hearts have opened
> and our dry bones live.

O God of love and mercy, you have promised to put your spirit
into our rattling bones.

> Let us never settle for the valley of dry bones.
>
> Breathe life into us, forgive us our despair, our hopelessness.
>
> Forgive us for believing that it all depends on us.
>
> We fail to acknowledge that you alone, O God,
> put breath in us and give us life.

Gracious God

> Continue to surprise us with images that open us to your truth.
>
> May we continue to be startled by your bold vision
> for a common humanity,
>
>> bones that live, the breath of live that gives us life.
>
> We confess that our embrace is too small, our bones too dry,
> our breath too shallow.
>
> Forgive us and embolden us to live boldly, to breathe deeply,
> to risk without fear.

✛

One of Chautauqua's most treasured preachers is the Rev. Dr. Fred Craddock. Few who were present would forget when he preached a series of sermons titled "The Gifted and Strong." Yes, that would be us.

In the face of a world in turmoil, we pray for ourselves,
    the gifted and strong, and we dare to face the responsibility of our gifts.
Almighty God, Giver of all gifts, Source of all strength,
    we give thanks for all that has been given to us.
    With humility and hesitation, we, gifted and strong,
    accept your call to use our gifts wisely
    and with generosity of heart and spirit.
God of history, yesterday, today and tomorrow,
    we face a future unknown to us.
    We pray for the courage and the imagination to offer ourselves
    and our gifts on behalf of all who seek peace
    and justice for your children.
    We pray for the humility to see our carefully laid plans as imperfect,
    our ideas as ever open to change.
    We pray for the gift of tenacity
    as we, the gifted and strong, dare to claim for our lives
        dreams that live beyond our years,
        beyond our own families.
    Inspire us to love generously, passionately and eternally.

✠

God of Justice, and Grace, and Mercy,
You have always called your people to be future pulled, not past driven.
    You invite us to be co-creators in a world that is of your making.
    You urge us to risk, even to fail, looking toward a future
    that is beyond our knowing.
With humility we pray for guidance as we risk setting forth our best ideas.
    We do so in full recognition that your future will always be marked
    by your love for the whole of creation.
    You care for every child created in your image.
With humility we pray for the courage to follow your will and your way.
    All who have walked the grounds of the place
    we lovingly call Chautauqua
    are touched by the beauty of this place.
    And almost all surprise themselves as they quietly,
    some with embarrassment,
    declare their experiences spiritual.
With humility we pray for a holy passion to claim minds and hearts
    as we move
    toward a future where success is measured
    by the finest in human values,
    a future of justice and mercy and love.
Finally we are moved to pray for a kinder future for all who suffer
    as they face the future armed with faith alone.
    We pray for ourselves that we might never lose our urge to reach out
    beyond our own familiar borders.
So with gratitude and humility we receive the many gifts
    that have been entrusted to our safe keeping.
Teach us, Holy One, to share!

✜

Surprise us with your presence, O God;
renew our sense of wonder.
Give us energy and courage to live as your people in this world.
In an incredibly insecure and uncertain world,
we thank you, God for the surprise
of our security and serenity,
for the gift of our abundance,
for the beauty that surrounds us.
How do we say thank you?

We are your blessed people, the gifted and strong.
Open our hearts that we might surprise ourselves
with generosity of spirit and boundless affection
even for those we do not know.
We, who have the capacity to make dreams reality,
grant us the courage to create a future of hope,
Not only for ourselves but for those unknown to us.
Let us live beyond the boundaries of limited imagination.

Surprise us with your presence, O God,
Renew our sense of wonder.
Give us energy and courage to live as your people in this world.
Amen.

✙

Loving God,

We come confessing that we sometimes have trouble seeking answers to problems, seeking relief for pain. We look to resources we can purchase, advice that can be bought, and the expert who might have the answers to the questions that confound us. Oh yes, we humbly confess that we would like to be seen as strong, fearless, problem free. We are the people of solutions and we pride ourselves on our well-ordered lives. But every now and then there is a stirring in our soul that cannot be easily quieted.

We confess that it is at that point when we pray, all too often without much hope that it will help.

But our God is a God of surprise.

Sometimes help comes from the most unlikely place; the hug of a tiny grandchild can relieve the pain born of loneliness. The words of the Charter of Compassion, meant to inspire the world, becomes for one troubled soul a vision, a solution beyond anger for deep pain and the hope for a bright faith-filled future. We confess that even as we hear the biblical stories read again and again we sometimes miss the word of truth, like the source of bread for the hungry in the hand of a small child, bread enough to feed five thousand.

Loving God, you are a God of surprises.

Open us to the surprises of your boundless love for each and all.

✣

Lord of the Dance,
Giver of all things lovely and life giving,
we dedicate today to your glory this place where creativity
is nurtured and treasured,
where young bodies and minds are tended and trained,
where beauty carefully crafted becomes available
to even those who watch.

Gracious God,
We give thanks today for the generosity of those who share
of who they are and what they have.
Teachers, dancers, patrons, and lavish donors,
Carol Hirsh, whose joyous and generous spirit
enabled dreams to become reality,
Patti and Jean-Pierre, whose lives have opened to the searching
a world that gives love.

God of all our tomorrows—we dedicate to you
our hopes and dreams.
We give thanks for the gifts we have been given,
for the years ahead that will be a blessing beyond our living.
Amen.[21]

✠

---

21. This prayer was written in dedication of Bonnefoux-McBride Studio, Chautauqua's dance studio. Carol Hirsh, who loves Chautauqua and all that it stands for, is a humble woman with a dream. Her financial contribution to the dance studio helped to turn a dream into reality. Her support for the Department of Religion has been equally as generous and we are grateful.

In preparation for the prayers of the people let us with deep revealing admit that neither pastor nor people know how to pray; yes, we know the words but to reach deep inside, to speak to one we do not see or whose answers we never really know, this is in truth a challenge. But the scripture speaks to us and in Romans comforts us with the assurance that it is our hearts that pray, our hearts that hear words of faith.

So likewise the Spirit helps us in our weakness, for we do not know how to pray as we aught but that very spirit intercedes with sighs too deep for words. And God, who searches our heart, knows what is in the mind of the Spirit because the spirit intercedes for the saints according to the will of God.

Let us risk now some quiet moments of silence that we might search our hearts and acknowledge that God knows our needs even before we speak.

> *Spirit of the living God, fall afresh on us.*
> *Meld us, mold us, fill us, use us.*
> *Spirit of the living God, fall afresh on us.*[22]

Loving God,
  Hear the prayers of your people spoken in silence—
  shared heart to heart.
      Hear now our corporate prayers
      As we share the life of our church today.
  We pray that our witnesses will be true to the teachings
  of the Holy One.
      Give us a voice for the silenced
      And quiet communion when only silence will honor pain.
      Give us tears in the face of grief
      And laughter as we experience the joy of your creation.

---

22. "Spirit of the Living God," words and music by Daniel Iverson, 1935, Moody Press, Moody Bible Institute of Chicago.

Give us sharpness in the revealing of injustice
And your eternal gentleness with those
who cross our paths in despair.
Give us discernment as we make decisions.

(Sing the hymn, "Spirit of the Living God.")

✠

Loving God,
Your reach is broad,
your vision bold,
your love deeper than the deepest ocean,
wider than the universe we know.
Forgive us the limits of our loving.
Forgive us the timidity of our vision.
Forgive us our special pleading,
reserving you for us and our kind.

Eternal God,
Your image lies in the hearts of all people.
You have given life to us and to people
whose ways are different from ours,
whose faiths are foreign to us,
whose languages are unintelligible to us.
Forgive us for claiming that we alone
have favor in your eyes.

Creator God,
You set the stars in the midnight sky,
you brought light into deepest darkness,
you brushed away the shadows where fear grows,
where bigotry and war and hatred are fed.
You sent us a child and love was born.
Peace was made possible.
Forgive us, O God,
the fears that reside in the deep recesses of our broken hearts.
Help us to recognize you in the words of truth,
the things of beauty, the actions of love around us.

✠

Creator God,
> We come today to ask your blessing on the Fowler-Kellogg Art Center.
> Much more that a beautiful structure, this work of art and imagination
> will be a witness to creativity and potential.

We dedicate this center that melds memories of lives too early lost,
> future dreams unfulfilled.

We give thanks for the generosity of those
> who have shared from their bounty
> that Chautauqua might offer to a world in search of meaning
> a place where dreams can be realized.

Gracious God,
> You have blessed this place with a spirit of kindness and caring.
> We are grateful and we dedicate this very special place to your glory.

May this Fowler-Kellogg Art Center serve as an inspiration now
> and for generations to come.
> Amen.[23]

---

23. This prayer was written for the dedication of the Fowler-Kellogg Art Center. The prayer recognizes much more than the dedication of a treasured building. This historic structure is the Fowler family's concrete remembrance of their young daughter, Angela Linn Fowler. She died much too young, her dreams unfulfilled. But in her short life, she loved, and was loved. So the Fowler-Kellogg Art Center stands as both tribute and inspiration for generations yet to come.

❈ 14 ❈

CHAUTAUQUA—BELOVED COMMUNITY

I t is entirely fitting that the opening prayer of this chapter, "Chautauqua —Beloved Community," is dedicated to Daniel Bratton, Chautauqua's fifteenth president, who served for sixteen years. Dan invited me to join the staff of Chautauqua in January of 2000. I remain grateful for his courage in bringing to Chautauqua the first woman to serve as director of the Department of Religion.

My mind wanders back to the time when Dan, full of vigor and excited about his coming retirement, introduced me as the new director of the Department of Religion. I felt very new and he made me feel very welcomed.

One year later, and then fully Chautauqua's pastor, I asked for prayers for Dan and his family as he faced the twilight of his life. Dan had been diagnosed with pancreatic cancer and it had metastasized to his liver. This was the medical diagnosis and it was not good news.

But Dan's spiritual diagnosis was as good as it gets. Dan was Dan—humor intact, secure is his faith, cradled in the arms of a family that loved him, concerned not about his future but his family's, and, yes, Chautauqua's. We were all in his prayers and we kept him in ours. Hear his words:

"Remember, that hope is a life force, that it is no assurance of living long, but for all the faithful, hope is our hallmark."

Dan's words said it all. "Joan, pray not for a miracle, for that is false hope, but for strength and courage for the Bratton family as we face a future unchartered. Make us a blessing to one another."

God, make our love a blessing to all your children everywhere. Grant us strength and courage for the days and hours, years and months given to us.

Live fully. Love well. Rejoice in all things.

REVERIE FOR DAN BRATTON

We remember, especially today, the family and colleagues of Daniel Lindsay Bratton. Dan Bratton, the fifteenth president of Chautauqua, served for sixteen years. Dan died at age sixty-eight on June 10, 2001, at dawn. His entry into immortality was punctuated with loud claps of thunder. Dan will be missed. His legacy is secure, and he now becomes part of the sacred memory of Chautauqua.

Let us pray.

Creator God, whose love for us is boundless,
whose ways are beyond our understanding,
whose creativity is beyond our imagining,
we come with humility, yet with high expectation.
We lay before you the concerns of our hearts.
We speak haltingly, for the anguish of our souls
lies too deep for words.
We open ourselves to you and share
our most hidden sorrows.
We pray today for all whose mornings begin
with pain born of illness or anxiety.
Touch each and every one with your healing power.
We pray for all your people around this wide world.
For those children who are born into loveless families,
for all who go to bed hungry,
who suffer from famine and flood,
for all who face the violence born of war and bigotry,
bring justice; grant peace.
Encourage our hearts that we might be in your service
until all are fed, housed, clothed, and freed.
In this moment of silence,
we speak now prayers for those we love
and even for ourselves,
who stand in need of your grace.
The storm has passed; the sun shines.
We are blessed, good and gracious God; we are grateful.

In a world of uncertainty and insecurity
we give thanks for a place called Chautauqua,
where small children play safely and grandparent's treasure
their generous hugs and enjoy their boundless energy.
In a world of breaking news there is here a timeless story,
a beauty that God, the creator, has crafted for us
and for the generations that are yet to come.
In a world of fear
Chautauqua offers the peace of faith.
We are gathered here, God's children, blessed beyond our own doing.
We express our heartfelt thanks for all that surround us.
We give thanks in full knowledge that for us food is always plentiful.
We pray for the day when all God's children
are fed and housed and clothed and freed.
Until that day this prayer of our hearts continues.

✟

God of our yesterdays, today, and all our tomorrows,
   Like those who came before us we dare to ask you,
   bless this very special place we call Chautauqua.
With humility we acknowledge that
   we hold in our hands something precious—
   a spirit-filled center that creates
   a place in our hearts that lasts for generations.
On this day of new beginnings
   we pray for the energy,
   the courage, and the passion
   needed to build for generations yet to be born
   a Chautauqua that will continue to inspire,
   to educate, and to transform those who journey here.
We pray as well for all who gather here this season
   and for those who will no longer be here with us.
   We pray for memories that live beyond life.
May the Chautauqua they have entrusted to our keeping
   grow and prosper in our time
   and by our hands.
God of surprises,
   Thank you, God, for the surprise of Chautauqua.
   Only you, O God, could have planned a place so beautiful,
   a place where the trees touch the stars
   and the waters of the lake washes the land,
   a lake that is home to sea creatures and plants and
   grants pleasure to children and sailors and ice fisherman alike.
We are grateful for all who have tended this gracious gift and pray
   for the wisdom and the insight to surprise generations yet unborn
   with this spiritual home that has blessed our lives.
God of surprises,
   Thank you, God, for the surprising gift of life.
   You have made each of us, marked us as distinct and different,
   hand-crafted and loved.
   We look at the infinite variety around us,
   all shades of color, all shapes and sizes, from many cultures,
   and the wonder of newborn life and the wisdom of age.

As we give thanks for this the greatest surprise of all,
we pray that you might stretch us to love all life,
to so invest ourselves in the protection of life
that all your children will one day be fed
and housed and clothed and free.
And for those for whom the heart has stopped beating
and breath has stilled,
we pray for your ultimate surprise, life beyond death.
Finally, O God, we await the surprise of the future you envision
for your people.
We pray that with the choices we make,
the decisions we and those who lead us set forward,
we will surprise you as we reach
toward your future of unity and justice and peace for all your people
in all the world.
And for the continuing surprise of your love for each of us,
even as we disappoint and delight,
we receive your love as gift and grace and always trust in you;
We are grateful beyond words.
Amen.

God of mystery and majesty,
>   The beauty of your creation surrounds us.
>   We praise in wonder at this admixture that stirs our complacent souls.
>   We do not fully understand the mystery of this place
>   and if we try too hard, the power of the unknowable escapes us.
>   We know that we are unable to recreate this miraculous gift
> that speaks to us
>   in the rustle of the leaves,
>   in the turmoil of the storm,
>   in the twinkle of each evening star.
>   All we know is that all this is a gift created by your majestic hand.
> Wonder of wonder—the gift is ours to receive and enjoy and cherish
>   from generation to generation.

✛

Affectionate, tireless God,
> whose love embraces the whole world,
> you never grow weary of our asking
> and we are grateful.

We pray today for families.
> We pray for the larger family that is Chautauqua.
> May we find in one another solace for our suffering,
> Grace in the face of our weakness,
> understanding when we are less than kind,
> faith to carry us through the darkest of days,
> and unrestrained joy in the laughter of our children.

We pray as well for every person's family gathered here,
> for grandparents, for mothers, fathers, partners, husbands, wives,
> ex-husbands, ex-wives, difficult relatives,
> discordant and broken relationships, new lovers, and lovers
> made whole in the crucial of years of living.
> For the gift of intimacy we say Amen.
> For the hope in the smiles of children,
> we are all softened and made tender.
> And for those who live alone,
> may the families you craft from friends bless your lives.

Now God of all that is and is to come, we pray for your people
the world around
> and if there is anything we can do,
> any sacrifice we might make,
> any action that might ease pain,
> open our hearts that we might love beyond our own.

God, on this glorious day where the sun blesses us
> who gather here, we pray for those who are absent.
> We ask for those in need of healing that they feel your special touch.
> For those for whom healing is not possible,
> and for those who grieve,
> we pray for peace.
> For the tie that binds us to one another we sing Alleluia!

✛

Prayer for Peace:
Spirit of God, descend upon our hearts.
    Help us to soften, to bend.
    Make us long to hear the story of how we can become peacemakers.
    Be with us as we experience our own humility and poverty of spirit.
    Hear us in our grief;
    encourage every spark of mercy kindled in us.
    Create in us the longing for right living.
    Shine light into the corners of our hearts so that we know
        where we still hold envy and jealousy and resentment,
    then sustain us as we try to right what we've toppled.
    Light of the world, light the path we are choosing to walk,
    the path that will, at each stepping place,
        be a testament to our commitment to tenderness and compassion.
Spirit of God, teach us to walk as peacemakers each moment of each day.
Creator God,
    We pray for those among us called artists, those whose
    creative spirits point us to a more excellent way.

Prayer for Artists:
    We remember all those to whom you have given special gifts
    to sing and paint, to sculpt and act, to dance and design.
    It is artists who ennoble the human spirit, who open us to our world
    by engaging bodies, minds, and hearts in new and special ways.
    Work through these creative ones
    whose gifts help us to grapple with life in the face of enormous tragedy,
    whose gifts help us to wrestle with upset and turmoil
    and relentless remembering.
    We thank you, Lord, for working through the artists.
Creator God,
    We offer our prayer for this place created by your hands
    long before we drew breath.

Prayer for Chautauqua:
Father God,
    You have blessed us with this place, crafted by your hand
    long before we drew breath.

We are humbled by beauty, trees, gardens, the lake,
historic architecture, a city beautiful.
We thank you for opportunity to live and work, play and worship
in this glorious setting.
Remind us to treasure Chautauqua, never to take it for granted.
We, your children, are stewards of this place, this lake, this air,
this land. Father God, help us.

Mother God,
As stewards of all that is Chautauqua, we seek your guidance
in the building of true community.
Here gather your people, diverse in race and creed,
ideas and choice of activities.
Thank you for your gift of our special identities.
All of us are created in your image,
each an expression of your many faces.
Help us, Mother God, to learn from each other.
Nurture us all as your children.

Yahweh,
We ask your special blessing for our leaders.
Grant them vision and patience.
Working together is not without stickiness.
With humility we ask, help us to listen well, speak thoughtfully,
Broaden our understanding on the many issues
that define our community.
Walk with us as we of different faiths reach out to one another.

Allah,
Blessed by a rich history,
help us to reach for a bold and faithful future.
Remind us of the generosity of spirit that created this place,
that brought us to this common altar.
Help us to grow in that spirit.

God, send us home to be Chautauquans in all the places we live.

God of eternity,
We pray for the children of the world, for their future,
that it might be bright with hope.

Prayer for the Future:

> God, I'm Katie. You knew me before I was born.
> You know I arrived in this world on September 11, 1989.
> I worry, God, about the future. I worry that for all the world's
> children born on September 11,
>> our birthday will always be remembered as a day of tragedy.
> We children pray that it will be the day when courage was born.
> God,
>> I know that your children all around this world want peace.
> Today, I pray on their behalf.
> I pray in the presence of parents and grandparents,
>> people who can help to chart the future.
>> Grant them strength and courage,
>> that they might leave to us a world where everyone
>> has enough to eat,
>> a safe place to sleep, a place where there is love
>> and forgiveness and hope.

Prayer for Ourselves:

> And now, precious Lord, take our hand as we reach out
> to one another.
> As we take our leave from one another, we ask especially
> that you hold us in your care.
> Hear the unspoken prayer of our hearts.
> Hold each one precious
> for whom we silently pray, and be with each and every one
> in the days and months to come.
> Amen.

✠

Good Shepherd,
> We come into this place made sacred by generations
> of prayer and praise.
>> We come to listen to your word in hymn and sermon.
>> We come into this blessed pasture to be fed
>>> the bread of life and love.
> We confess that though these are our
>> most heartfelt desires,
>> our minds wander and fill with private worries.
>> we fail to believe that you will comfort us
>>> if only we acknowledge:

We are God's people, the flock of the Lord.

Good Shepherd,
> We come today blessed by our time together here at Chautauqua.
>> We prepare to take leave of this safe, sensitive, and
>>> Spirit-filled place.
>> We fear that as we move back to work and competition,
>>> busyness and tension,
>>> we may lose our way.
>> We confess that we fail to internalize your promise
>>> that you go with us in every moment of our lives,
>>> in love and laughter, tears, anger, jealousy,
>>> study, sacrifice, suffering,
>>> and even death.
>> Yea, though we walk through the deepest valley,
>>> the most frightening shadow,
>> We who confess our fears,
>>> Receive your promises.

We are God's people, the flock of the Lord.

Good Shepherd,
> You call us to follow you.
> You remind us we are your flock,
>> all of us, every child, rich or poor, of every color,
>> language, gender, sexual orientation.

We confess that we, your people,
    have divided and subdivided
    and divided ourselves again and again.
We want too often to create our own flock
    so we can be the shepherd.
We confess we seek to be shepherd
    in flocks of our own making.
We fail to humbly acknowledge that we are your flock,
    and you are our Shepherd.

We are God's people, the flock of the Lord.

We make here our confession in the sure knowledge
    that even if we stray from your way,
    you promise to find us and love us back to obedience
and compassion and humility. Amen.

✠

Gracious God,
    As we offer our season end thanks, our gratefulness to you
    is too deep for words,
        too close to our hearts to give our feelings voice.
    That we have Chautauqua to help our spirits soar
    is a gift beyond our imagining.
    Only you, O God, could have planned a place so beautiful,
        a place where the trees touch the stars
        and the waters of the lake refresh the land,
        a lake that is home to water creatures and plants and
        grants pleasure to children and sailors and ice fishermen alike.
    We are grateful for all who have tended this gift and pray
        for the wisdom and the insight to surprise generations yet unborn
        with this spiritual home that has blessed our lives.
Creator God, thank you for the gift of life.
    You have made each of us, marked us distinctly,
    handcrafted us, and loved us.
    We look at the infinite variety around us, all shades of color,
    all shapes and sizes, all ages.
    We marvel at the wonder of newborn babies,
    at the energy of children and the wisdom of age.
    We give thanks for life, which is the greatest surprise of all.
    We pray that you might stretch us to love all life,
    to seek anew your will and your way,
        so to invest ourselves in the protection of all your children
        that one day they will be fed and housed and clothed and free.
Now with the deepest reverence
    we pray for those for whom the heart has stopped beating
    and breath has stilled.
    We pray for them your ultimate surprise, life beyond death.
    Even in the pain we glimpse joy beholding how your grace
    is still unfolding,
        give us your vision, God of love.
Ever present God, as we depart from one another,
    we pray for our common future and put our faith
    in the future you envision for your people.

We pray for our nation, especially at this crossroad
and this time of decision.
We pray for the vulnerable in every land that they might know
security and dignity and justice.
We place ourselves in your hands and dare to pray your will be done
on this earth as it is done in heaven.
Give us strength to love each other, Spirit of Kindness.
Be our guide.
Now on this special day we pray for those who suffer,
    for those with strained family relations,
    for those who bear secrets or sadness,
    for those who are ill and for those who care for them,
    for those whose eyes have closed to this life on earth;
    we pray as well for those who await surgery
    and for those who face long months of recovery.
We pray especially for those seeking to serve your people as
elected officials.
Grant them wisdom; grant them courage.
In our hearts we know that our prayers are for all,
named and unnamed, known and unknown.
We pray for all that is yet to be; we put our future in your hands.
You who know each thought and feeling,
teach us all your way of healing.
Give us peace beyond our fear and hope beyond our sorrows.
Now let us say together the prayer that travels with us
beyond these days, beyond these gates:

Recite the Lord's Prayer in unison.

On this our final Sunday morning worship,
    We part from one another.
    We go now to those congregations we call home.
As your summer pastor, I say to you,
as God's own,
    clothe yourself with compassion,
    kindness, patience,

forgiving all who disappoint you
as God has forgiven you.
Crown all things with love,
which binds everyone together in perfect harmony.
Go now in peace to love and serve.

✛